24% MORE

The Advice & Advisor Every Company Owner Needs

JOHN LANGSTON, CAIA, MBA

Founder and CEO, Republic Capital Group

Langston Wealth Management Center at
McCOMBS SCHOOL OF BUSINESS
The University of Texas at Austin

SILVERSMITH
PRESS

Published by Silversmith Press—Houston, Texas
www.silversmithpress.com

Cover Design by Target Marketing Digital New York, New York

ISBN 978-1-967386-03-1 (Hardcover Book)
ISBN 978-1-967386-01-7 (Softcover Book)
ISBN 978-1-967386-02-4 (eBook)

Disclaimer:

The information contained in this book is for general educational and informational purposes only. The opinions expressed herein are solely those of the author, a registered representative of a FINRA member firm, and do not necessarily reflect the views of the firm.

Nothing in this book should be construed as personalized financial advice, investment advice, or a recommendation to buy or sell any securities. The author is not providing financial planning, legal, or tax advice. You should consult with a qualified financial advisor, tax professional, or attorney before making any financial decisions.

Investing in securities involves risks, and there is always the potential for loss. Past performance is not indicative of future results.

For more information about the author, please visit FINRA BrokerCheck at brokercheck.finra.org.

*To my wife and soulmate, Candace:
I love you. Thank you for loving me and
never thinking anything is too big to accomplish
if we are helping others and God is helping us.*

CONTENTS

SPECIAL THANKS

To my parents, Larry and Diann Langston, I am extremely proud to be your son. Thank you for modeling how to love and help others and for loving and helping me.

To my Republic Capital Group team, you are awesome at investment banking, but you are even better people. Thank you for everything you have done to make Republic successful.

To Blake Cargill, you believed before it came to be and you are the best Robin a Batman could ask for.

To our clients across the country, Republic exists because of your trust in us, and we are grateful.

To the Langston Fellows and students at the Langston Wealth Management Center at the University of Texas McCombs School of Business, you are all so bright and are the future of how wealth will be managed in our world. Never forget that true wealth is having the time, health, and capital to pursue the purpose you were born for. Your purpose uses the strengths you were born with and is for the betterment of others. I believe in you!

To my children, John David, Savannah, Stephen,

Zachary, Rachel, Austin, Sadie, and Preslie, I'm so very proud of you and how you treat others. I love you completely and unrelentingly.

To my siblings Jesse, Daniel, Carissa, and Carrie, we were the original ones who figured things out together, and built businesses together. Your support and love has meant so much to me and we aren't done yet.

To Frankie Mazzapica my friend of 31 years, and Pastor for the last 16 years, thank you for invaluable advice and support at crucial times, it's made a world of difference. You are a brother to me.

Soli Deo gloria!

THE MUST-READ PART
MORE THAN MONEY

You might be curious about this book's title: 24% *More*. It comes from research showing that company owners who work with an experienced M&A investment banker can increase the value of their company's sale by an average of twenty-four percent.

In the chapters ahead, I'll show you exactly how that happens—not just in theory, but in real dollars and cents. More importantly, I'll show you how the right investment banker doesn't just add value to your transaction, they can add value to your entire life's journey.

My goal is for you to walk away from these pages with a clear understanding of what investment bankers do—specifically those who specialize in helping clients buy and sell companies. More importantly, I want you to see why trying to sell your company on your own is a risk you don't want to take. It's a path filled with costly pitfalls that can lower your company's value, waste your time, and create life-altering stress you never saw coming.

All this is true whether you are seeking to sell all or part of your company.

To be honest though, this book isn't really about money. It's about something much greater. Money is just a tool. What you do with it is what really matters.

The insights in this book work best when your advisor—and you—value people over money, fame, or personal achievement.

Now, I'm not naive. We all have personal motives—and that's not a bad thing. We all need to survive, grow, provide for our families, plan for the future, and meet our own emotional needs. But I've learned this: putting people first is what matters most. Time and time again, I've seen that when you consistently lead with care, respect, and service to others, you become more valuable—not just in business, but in every area of life.

The goal of this book ultimately is to help you achieve *your* purpose.

Money isn't the purpose—it's the fuel *for* your purpose. It's a reward for hard work and risk-taking, and it's a tool to make an impact on others. If this book helps you take positive steps toward achieving your purpose, then I'll be fulfilling mine.

Years ago, I attended a workshop with Dr. Kevin Elko. He's famous for coaching top corporations, athletes and teams such as Emmitt Smith, the Dallas Cowboys, the Philadelphia Eagles and Tyson Foods. He asked us to write down our life purpose in one short phrase. Today, I still have the small card with my response—fifteen years and multiple moves later. It simply says: "Help advisors, help people." At that time, they were my sole clients. Over the years I've simplified my purpose to "Help people" although much of my work is still done alongside financial advisors.

Living with the purpose of "helping people" has had a tremendous impact on my life. Time and again, I've started a relationship or negotiation thinking, *How can I help this person?* This has led to my most meaningful career wins. Sometimes it seems as if I have a secret superpower to see all the pieces falling into place; but I definitely don't. What I've realized is that when you pursue a purpose beyond yourself—like helping others—the wind is at your back, the sun shines on you, and the currents push you forward instead of fighting against you.

Here's the way I see it: you can build a sailboat, but you can't make the wind. I've discovered that when you pursue the purpose of helping others, you'll find the wind blowing in your sails. In other words, something intangible is added to your efforts. Yes, be proud that you "built the boat" but also be grateful for the wind. No human being sent you that wind, or the sun, or the rain for your garden. My father always said, "If you see a turtle on a fence post, you know it didn't get there on its own." Well, I see myself as that turtle. I've been lifted by others and pushed along by the wind.

So, as you read about the economic, mental, and emotional benefits of working with an investment banker, remember this: It's all about helping you accomplish your purpose because in the end, that's what really matters most.

CHAPTER 1

THE GAPING HOLE IN MODERN FINANCIAL PLANNING

Modern financial planning has meaningfully improved the way wealth is managed in the world today. In the past, financial advisors were primarily focused on investments for clients but today there is more of a holistic, client-centric approach that is benefiting clients greatly. I've observed the changes over the years and actually started my career as a financial advisor. The firm I was with at the time was intensely planning-focused, more so than just about any other firm I knew. We used a comprehensive twenty-eight-page document to evaluate our clients' goals and current financial situation. I enjoyed this work and excelled at it, but I eventually left to spend a season working in the non-profit world before returning to the industry.

Today, high-quality, planning-focused firms are coordinating multiple disciplines such as tax and legal planning alongside the broader services of financial planning. This higher coordination drives much better outcomes for their clients and saves them a lot of time. The financial advisor can help "quarterback" key deliverables and act as a guide for the overall financial, tax, and legal plan execution. As a busy company owner dealing with a lot of complexity, this skillful coordination has been a huge benefit. I'm an unabashed fan of what modern financial planning can do HOWEVER . . . there is still a gaping hole in the industry today.

"HEY, WHAT ABOUT MY LARGEST ASSET?"

Despite all the ways modern financial planners are helping, many are not encouraging company owners to get the advice of a professional investment banker specializing in mergers and acquisitions (M&A) to help them devise a proper exit strategy—potentially the biggest financial decision they will ever make. These professionals help company owners buy and sell companies, and advise on how to maximize the value of a company.

One day, I was in New York City meeting with an accomplished and renowned private equity investor. He and his firm have made some outstanding investments, and he is well regarded in the financial services industry. We were discussing this idea that modern financial planning does not consider or effectively address the private company ownership many clients have, and he shared a personal story with me. He told me he met with a top-tier financial institution that took a substantial amount of time to investigate his goals, discuss his risk tolerance, and get to know him which he really appreciated. Then they presented him with their portfolio recommendation: sixty percent invested in equities and forty percent invested in bonds. For a healthy executive in his forties, this would normally be a very common recommendation. He then asked where in the analysis they had taken into account that ninety percent of his current wealth was allocated to private equity holdings, given his ownership of a private equity firm. Their blank looks answered the question. They hadn't considered it at all.

Unfortunately, I have had similar conversations with owners of large private real estate holdings who were advised to include publicly-traded real estate as part of their investment portfolio. Now, to be clear, I likely have friends who are financial planning professionals who would say, "Our team would never make those mistakes," and they are right. Their teams are skilled and dedicated to their clients. But I invite you to consider a recent situation I encountered. We took on a client who had completed the most extensive estate planning I have ever seen. He worked closely with some of the most wealthy and famous people in the world and he had witnessed the fallout of just handing wealth over to their children and it troubled him greatly. He was deeply concerned about making sure that his children would find a meaningful purpose in life and that the windfall of their inheritance would not take away their drive. His net worth was well over $100 million before taking into account his company ownership. He believed his company was worth around $85 million dollars and planned accordingly. Ultimately, we sourced and closed an investor in his company at a valuation of $124 million dollars—that's forty-seven percent more than he and his advisors had planned for!

Of course, he was pleased and recently told me that the equity he accepted from the new investor in the overall company was the best investment of his life.

My point is that financial planners and their clients need a market-based understanding of the company's value and the strategic insight an investment banking firm can provide. There are so many ways to benefit clients by understanding their private company ownership better. A firm like ours doesn't just help with transactions; we assist in developing strategy around ways to maximize the company's performance in many areas. The ultimate measure of a company's health and outlook is its enterprise value. We help companies execute many facets that affect enterprise value. For example, our Enterprise Advisory Division helps with things like succession planning. They have been involved in thousands of employee succession events and many mergers that require strategic planning and execution.

Sometimes, financial terms are different than they initially appear, and we coordinate with our client's financial advisors to ensure the value is maximized for our mutual client.

This happens when you consider all the factors impacting a sale, and especially taxation. For example, the owner of a company I represented was debating multiple offers, and one of the offers was prepared to close and transact before year-end. The other buyers needed more time and were not focused on making the purchase before year-end. We reviewed the situation with the client's financial advisor. He noted that the owner had significant losses from other investments, and tax law changes for the next year would negatively impact our client. The client could carry the losses forward and deduct them against gains if he did so before year-end. This made the offer that was prepared to close quickly the most attractive by a fair amount.

This is one example of why it's so important to have outstanding coordination between the investment banker and the financial advisor.

Unfortunately, in many cases, professional advisors are not coordinating the way they should. This is a big mistake, and we make every effort to work closely with all your professional advisors in our process.

A good financial advisor will build a complete roadmap of your financial situation. They'll cover taxes, estate planning, and asset protection. They'll also discuss how selling your company will affect your personal finances. At Republic Capital Group, we work with many of the top financial advisors in the United States and we have seen firsthand the value they bring to clients. They handle the finances and estate planning. They also work with lawyers to set up the needed legal structures.

When you think about the coordination of the team, there are three key aspects to consider:

1. QUARTERBACK OF A CLIENT'S PLANNING: A GREAT ADVISOR

A great financial advisor acts as the quarterback of your liquid assets and the factors that affect your financial life. There are various business models within the financial or wealth management industry, and it's essential to recognize the type of model you are currently in as a company owner.

The key is whether the professional you work with cares about your overall picture, including investments, taxes, and estate planning. It's more strategic than just which stock, bond, mutual fund, or ETF to invest in.

Some models will provide in-house services like tax preparation and estate planning coordination with in-house legal help. Others will act as a quarterback, connecting and coordinating with outside firms, such as with your attorney about your estate plan. Either quarterbacking approach can work well.

To be candid, your financial advisors must see the entire picture. If they don't, they will be of little or no help in selling your company or raising capital.

At Republic Capital Group, we work with financial advisors to create a complete picture of our clients' financial lives the day after the transaction closes. We want to ensure you get good advice—*after* the transaction—about the planning, tax, and estate impacts of the big financial windfall coming your way.

2. YOUR ESTATE PLAN IS LIKELY TO CHANGE QUICKLY

A company sale or capital increase will likely transform your estate plan. You'll want to speak with your tax advisor, attorney, financial advisor, and others to update your plan. There are sometimes tax-saving opportunities we, as investment bankers, will not know about. We need to know the history of your other financial investments to guide you appropriately. We do not advise you on your entire investment portfolio, and it would not be appropriate for us to do so. We aren't here to replace your other advisors—we're here to work alongside them.

An effective investment banker has the humility to know when to advise and when to step back. When you're interviewing potential investment bankers, ask about their comfort level working with other professionals. If they act disdainfully toward other disciplines such as investments, tax, charitable giv-ing, or estate planning, that should be a red flag.

3. A GOOD FINANCIAL ADVISOR AND THEIR TEAM CAN COORDINATE THE DETAILS

At Republic Capital Group, we like to work in con-cert with professional and skilled financial advisors. They can help us find opportunities in our client's company's investment portfolio. We can also work with them on our client's philanthropic goals and help structure the deal to align with the overarching financial plan.

Also, many advisors now consider asset protec-tion and how your life might change. No one expects divorce, serious illness, a child entering into a less-than-ideal marriage, and so on. A sizable increase in your wealth from a company deal could change your financial planning needs in every area. Smart planning can help you avoid heartache down the road.

We welcome the opportunity to facilitate all these conversations with your financial advisor. A great transaction is like a three-legged stool: an investment banker, a financial advisor, and legal counsel. They must work together, communicate, and be aware of the details that must be coordinated.

CHAPTER 2
THE KEY TO FINDING CLARITY

As an investment banker specializing in mergers and acquisitions, I've spent two decades guiding company owners through the process of selling their companies. I've handled deals of all sizes and have witnessed and nurtured countless transactions, each unique in their own way. Each had its own challenges and opportunities, requiring the kind of adaptable approach described in these pages.

I've written this book to guide would-be sellers through the complex process of selling all or part of a company. By telling my story as an experienced investment banker, I hope you will find ideas to apply to your business and future opportunities.

You see, one factor consistently stands out as the key to success across all deals: *clarity.* The best deals happen when a company and its owners gain clarity about what they really want and what their actual options are. Have you ever had someone ask you what you want to eat while on a road trip in an unfamiliar area? You might have something in mind, but usually the answer is: "What are the choices?" Then once you select a restaurant, you look at the menu, and when you see your options, then you can finally decide what to eat. The key to clarity is to have a menu!

Most of us frequent the same drive-thru restaurants and each time we stop and look at the menu. We often order the same thing but we want to double check our options. The investment banker's role is to help orchestrate clarity by creating a menu of choices. The reason you aren't sure about what you want is because you haven't been presented with a menu, and you can't make a final decision about your company without knowing all your choices. I'll share more about the importance of clarity in a moment.

First, know that this book is written for three types of company owners:

1. **Those who are *ready* to sell all or part of their company.** These owners know their company needs capital and would like to sell part of it, or they have reached a point where they want to sell the entire company and pursue a new adventure, or perhaps retire.

2. **Those who are *considering* selling all or part of their company.** These owners have carefully reviewed and explored their *written* options to raise capital by selling part or all their company

but based on viable, actual options, have decided this isn't the right time to do so.

3. **Those who have not made *either* decision because they lack the information to know what step to take next.** They are troubled by this uncertainty and often contemplate what they should do. They read articles, talk to friends, and search the Internet for answers, yet they haven't decided anything. By not deciding, they are not considering what will happen to their company's future, to their company partners, and even their family if they don't sell at least some of the company.

As we've seen, black swan events like COVID or the Great Recession of 2007 can come along at any time and upend our best laid plans. Sometimes you can "stay too long at the fair" and wait to get even more money for your company than you could today. But what you'll learn in these pages is that if you sell your company the right way, you could get far more today than you might ever have imagined.

Now, as I mentioned previously, the key to making good decisions is having *clarity*. Many owners spend years debating what might happen if they sell their company based on subjective information or data. I can't think of many things less effective than trying to use data created in the past to guess what will happen with a particular business sale in the future.

Most privately-owned companies are unique—so unique, in fact, that their financial value often can't be accurately assessed with a simple analysis alone.

I always encourage owners to go through the investment banking process that I'll describe in detail in this book. The concrete information that *real written offers* provide will give you all the clarity you need to decide about the next chapter in your life.

THE THREE CRITICAL POINTS OF CLARITY

Most company owners considering selling all or part of their company lack clarity on three critical points:

1. How much will I really get?
2. How much of the company should I sell?
3. What role, if any, do I want after the sale?

As an investment banker, I recognize the uncertainty company owners feel when they lack clarity on these critical issues. The reason company owners often turn to Republic Capital Group is that we don't say, "Come to us when you have these things worked out." Instead, we say, "Let's work together to figure these issues out." Chances are, if you've met with an investment banker in the past, that banker told you to come back when you had made decisions about those three critical questions. But in reality, how can you make those decisions without the right information? That's why we say, let's figure these things out together.

Let's explore those three essential questions now.

HOW MUCH WILL I REALLY GET?

We've seen company owners who were not represented by a competent investment banker receive valuations up to thirty percent below their company's true market value. Your company may be worth a hundred million dollars to the right buyer, but you're being told that it's only worth seventy-five million. That's a huge disparity between what you're being offered and what your company is worth. Twenty five million dollars is a lot of money to leave on the table. How can you make a smart decision about selling if you're working from numbers that are so deeply flawed?

This discrepancy between what you're told your company is worth and its actual value occurs for several reasons. First, many company owners rely on outdated or incomplete information when estimating their company's value. They might look at industry averages or compare themselves to a competitor who recently sold their business. But they fail to consider the unique aspects of their company that could impact its value.

Secondly, company owners often underestimate the importance of intangible assets. While financial statements can give you a clear picture of your tangible assets, they don't capture the full value of things like your brand, company reputation, customer relationships, or proprietary processes. These intangible assets can dramatically increase your company's value in the eyes of potential buyers.

Lastly, many company owners don't fully understand how different deal structures can impact the final value they receive. For instance, an all-cash offer might seem attractive, but a deal that includes equity in the acquiring company could potentially yield a higher long-term return.

At Republic Capital Group, we conduct a comprehensive valuation, considering all the factors I just mentioned. We use sophisticated financial models, compare companies across an industry, and provide a realistic range of what your company might be worth in the current market.

But we don't stop there.

We then take this valuation to the market. We approach potential buyers to get real, written offers. Only when you have these concrete offers in hand can you truly understand what your company is worth in the marketplace. I keep coming back to *real written offers* because everything else is just theory and not something you can bank on or more importantly— put in the bank!

HOW MUCH OF THE COMPANY SHOULD I SELL?

Next, a company owner might be deciding whether to sell thirty percent, sixty percent, or all of the company. Or maybe it's some other percentage, but we'll use these three as examples. Again, we don't say, "Figure it out and get back to us." Instead we say, "Let's figure it out together. Let's get you actual options. What if you sold thirty percent? How much money or equity would you get? Or what about selling sixty percent? What would that get you?" And so on. Until you have those actual offers in hand—until you have clarity about your choices—how can you possibly make the best decision about how much to sell?

The decision about how much of your company to sell is about more than just money. It's about your goals, your lifestyle preferences, your vision for the future of the company, your legacy, and your plans. These considerations are essential because some experts suggest that the average company owner has between seventy and ninety percent of their net worth locked up in their business.

Let's examine some common scenarios.

SELLING A MINORITY STAKE (30% OR LESS)

Selling a minority stake can be an attractive option if you're looking to raise capital and grow your company while maintaining majority control. This approach can bring in both money and valuable partners who offer expertise and connections to help your company grow.

Bringing in minority investors, however, will change the way you run your company. You'll need to consider their input in major decisions, and you may need to implement more formal reporting and governance structures.

True, it wouldn't be *just your company* anymore, but you would also have one or more new allies in your quest for success.

SELLING A MAJORITY STAKE (51% TO 99%)

Selling a majority stake allows you to cash out a significant portion of your equity while still maintaining some ownership and involvement in the company. This can be a good option if you want to reduce your financial risk and command a higher valuation, as investors will often pay more for this larger stake. When you sell a majority stake, you're typically handing over a fair amount of legal control of the company.

The specifics can vary greatly, however, depending

on the deal structure and the buyer. Some buyers might want you to stay on in a leadership role, while others might prefer to bring in their own management team. As you'll see, private equity managers tend to prefer keeping owners involved for a specific period to boost company value and improve continuity. But other buyers may be competitors who want to roll your business into their operations and culture. It largely depends on how both sides can work together.

SELLING THE ENTIRE COMPANY (100%)

Selling your entire company provides the cleanest break and typically the largest immediate payout. If you're ready to retire or move on to a new venture, this can be the right choice. According to a 2023 report by the International Business Brokers Association (IBBA), retirement is the number one reason sellers go to market across all business sectors.[1]

A company owner must be emotionally and financially prepared for this transition, however. Until they have clarity about the next phase of their lives, many company owners cannot quantify the emotional impact of walking away from the company they've built literally from the ground up. I've worked with

---

1   International Business Brokers Association. *Market Pulse Report: Q3 2023 Executive Report.* November 2023. Accessed on October 29, 2024. https://www.ibba.org/wp-content/uploads/2023/11/mp_q3_2023_executive-report.pdf

sellers who were lukewarm at first—until they saw real, written offers. That's when they could finally envision a new life and became fully comfortable stepping into it.

At Republic Capital Group, we help company owners explore all options. We model out different scenarios, showing not only the financial implications but also how each option might impact your lifestyle and long-term financial goals.

WHAT ROLE, IF ANY, DO I WANT AFTER THE SALE?

Finally, many company owners say, "I don't want to work for someone else. No way." But when we bring our clients clarity about what their roles might be, sometimes they get very excited. They might have the chance to align with a larger enterprise they respect and still manage their current company without interference from above—while also putting a big check in the bank.

The role a company owner plays post-sale can vary widely, depending on the buyer and the deal structure. However, research shows that many owners fail to engage in any formal planning before striking a deal.

No matter where you are or what the size of your business is, it's important to think ahead. So, let's look at a few common scenarios about a company owner's possible.

COMPLETE EXIT

In some cases, particularly in 100 percent sales, the buyer may want a clean break. The seller might be asked to stay on for a short transition period but after that, is free to pursue other interests.

CONTINUED LEADERSHIP

Many buyers, especially financial buyers like private equity firms, prefer to keep the existing management team in place. The reason is simple: They want to ensure the continuity of the company's culture and leverage the seller's industry knowledge. In addition, incumbent management is a driver of value creation. The seller might be asked to stay on as CEO or in another leadership role, often with equity incentives tied to the company's future performance.

ADVISORY ROLE

Some deals might involve you stepping back from day-to-day operations but remaining involved in a strategic advisory capacity. This role can offer the best of both worlds—the freedom to pursue other interests while still contributing to the company you built.

EARN-OUT PERIOD

Sometimes, part of the purchase price might be tied to the company's performance over a certain period after the sale. In these situations, you might be required to stay involved to some degree to ensure a smooth transition and continued performance.

The key is to think carefully about what you want your life to look like after the sale: Do you want to stay involved in the company? Are you ready to retire? Do you have other ventures you want to pursue? Your answers to these questions should guide your decisions about what role, if any, you want after the sale.

THE IMPORTANCE OF QUALIFIED OFFERS

One of my client stories perfectly illustrates why clarity often comes—not from theory—but from real opportunities and engagement with the marketplace.

As we discussed the various potential buyers for my client's company, he mentioned one very prominent firm and said, "One firm I don't want to sell my company to is X."

I asked, "Why is that?"

He replied, "Well, the founder of the firm and I used to compete. I just can't see myself selling to him. We were always competing against one another and trying to win clients."

"Well, they're a very good firm," I replied. "I know

the founder personally. I'm not trying to influence you unduly, but I think it would be wise to at least talk to them. Perhaps their offer can be a comparison to other firms that you will consider."

Fortunately, he took my advice and allowed the investment banking process to move forward with his former competitor.

We did some preparation work, had a few calls with various potential buyers, and then scheduled a call with the founder of the one firm my client said he would never consider.

After the conference call ended, my client called me and said, "I hate how much I like that guy."

And, of course, you can probably guess the end of the story. After many conversations and seven very strong written offers, it became crystal clear to my client that the best path forward was with the very competitor he once ruled out.

A year later, he called me from Africa to thank me for helping him achieve the goal of a lifetime. He was on a safari with his entire family, and they were having a wonderful time connecting with each other and seeing amazing wildlife. He was also giving generously to support the poor through his religion, and he felt a tremendous sense of fulfillment and wanted to thank me for helping him achieve this goal. It was very gratifying for me as his investment banker.

This story illustrates a crucial point: *our preconceptions and emotions can cloud our judgment.* It's only by going through the process of getting actual offers and having real conversations with potential buyers that we can gain the clarity needed to make the best decision.

EMOTIONS DECIDE AND MINDS CONFIRM

Daniel Kahneman won the Nobel Prize in Economic Sciences in 2002. His research developed the Prospect Theory, which delves into the way people make decisions when facing financial risk. The theory is that people don't choose the most advantageous path, but instead focus on possible or perceived changes in gains or losses, which are often short-term and emotional in nature. This is why clarity is key. Your mind won't process information correctly and make a good decision until you are evaluating a real opportunity. Real written offers are the foundation of good selling decisions.

As you evaluate these offers, you'll eliminate the subjectivity, fears, anxieties, hopes, and dreams that your mind grapples with in the absence of concrete information. Instead, you'll confront your emotions with realistic paths forward.

My clients may be struggling with the fundamental question of what they want. They are freed from the prison of uncertainty when they receive clearly-defined options in the form of written offers. Not only are they clear about what to do next from an intellectual standpoint, but they are emotionally aligned with their final decision. Their excitement grows as they find comfort in having both mental and emotional alignment about their future.

WHY PROFESSIONAL GUIDANCE MATTERS

You might wonder why you need an investment banker to help you through this process. Can't you just figure it out on your own? Of course, it's possible to sell a company without professional help. But data shows that doing so often leaves significant value on the table. Remember that statistic I mentioned earlier—that many company owners receive valuations well below their company's true value? If your valuation is way below the actual worth of the company, how will you get that 24% *More*? The answer is you won't. That's where professional guidance can make a crucial difference.

In this book, I'll share with you a wide range of ideas that you need to be familiar with as a company owner. But I'll start with the most basic things I highlight for anyone learning about buying and selling businesses today. An experienced investment banker like me brings several key advantages to the table.

- **Market Knowledge:** We have our finger on the pulse of the M&A market. We know who's buying, what they're looking for, and what they're willing to pay.

- **Negotiation Expertise:** Selling a company is a complex negotiation. We know how to structure deals to maximize value and protect your interests.
- **Process Management:** Selling a company is a full-time job. We manage the process from start to finish, allowing you to focus on running your company.
- **An Emotional Buffer:** Selling a company can be emotional. We provide an objective perspective and can handle difficult conversations with potential buyers.
- **Broad Access to Buyers:** We have established relationships with a wide network of potential buyers, including strategic institutions and financial investors.

To illustrate the value we can bring, let me repeat that all-important statistic: *24% More.*

According to a 2014 study conducted at Alabama University and Portland State University, companies that engaged investment bankers received valuations twenty-four percent higher than those that sold independently.[1]

---

[1]   Agrawal, Anup and Cooper, Tommy and Lian, Qin and Wang, Qiming, Does Hiring M&A Advisers Matter for Private Sellers? (January 24, 2023). Quarterly Journal of Finance, Forthcoming, Available at SSRN: https://ssrn.com/abstract=2400531 or http://dx.doi.org/10.2139/ssrn.2400531

That's nearly a quarter more value unlocked for the company owners!

As I've said, my goal in this book is to help you find clarity as you consider selling your company. I want to help you focus on what's most important so that you can make the best possible decision.

REPUBLIC CAPITAL GROUP

In 2015, I was working for a Houston-based firm in financial services and I saw an opportunity. There was an unmet need in wealth management for someone to do traditional investment banking and focus on transactions.

There were a lot of consulting groups who would provide you with a valuation—and obviously, that's some of the work investment banks do. But it's not their core business; it's not why they exist. They exist to help firms do transformational things.

In September of 2015, I launched Republic Capital Group, a firm focused on helping wealth management firms with investment banking and investments. We were able to get the company off the ground because a sizable global firm was one of our very first clients. They paid us a large retainer—half a million dollars annually.

GROWING QUICKLY AND WINNING AWARDS

As we built the firm, we gained momentum. In 2019, we completed a landmark transaction in Beverly Hills, California. That deal went on to win Financial Services M&A Transaction of the Year at the M&A Advisor Awards.

In 2022 and 2023, we advised on more wealth management assets transactions than any other investment bank in our space. Of course, the giants in the field, like Goldman Sachs and Bank of America, did more—but none of our "competitors" got even close.

In the latter part of 2022, we helped one of the largest firms in this space acquire an accounting firm to provide better tax services. This turned out to be the largest acquisition of a CPA firm we know of in wealth management history. That year, we swept the M&A Advisor Awards, winning M&A Deal of the Year for all categories, and the most coveted award of all: Boutique Investment Banking Firm of the Year.

"START SPREADIN' THE NEWS . . ."

In mid-2023, I decided to move our headquarters from Houston to Rockefeller Plaza in New York City, and the benefits of that move have been extraordinary. We've successfully attracted superb local New

York talent. In addition, our visibility in the financial services world has increased dramatically.

Today, we also have partners in Chicago, Houston, Dallas, and West Palm Beach, and we pride ourselves on offering the best qualities all these great cities embody: Wall Street strategy for Main Street company owners.

WHO DO WE SERVE?

Most of our clients are closely-held private companies worth anywhere from $25 million to $500 million, built through hard work and grit. Some of the companies are owned by families who have worked closely together. Their legacy—as a family and a company—are very important to them.

It may surprise you to learn that thirty-five percent of Fortune 500 companies are family controlled.[1] Research done by Pepperdine University shows that family-owned companies are more valuable and more successful than other companies. However, data shows that few family businesses last past the third generation. Just 40% of family-owned businesses survive and pass on to the second generation, according to figures compiled by *Businessweek* and Cornell University in 1999 and

---

1   Dorsey, Vikki, "Impact of a family council intervention on owner knowledge and stewardship within a family business" (2015). *Theses and Dissertations*. 580. https://digitalcommons.pepperdine.edu/etd.

1987, respectively.[1] Those figures remained consistent into 2023, according to the Family Business Institute.[2] They also show that just thirteen percent extend to the third generation.[3]

ADDRESSING COMMON OBJECTIONS

Some company owners object to the idea of hiring an investment banker to handle the sale of their company. They're usually reluctant because of the same character qualities that made them successful entrepreneurs in the first place: They are hands-on leaders, doers, and go-getters.

If you are one of these folks, I get it, believe me. But let me ask you this: Would you sell your own house? Of course, you wouldn't. You have neither the time to get bogged down in the sale of your home nor, in most cases, the specific expertise to get the best offer.

Some people balk at the potential cost of hiring professional help. If that's your sticking point, let

---

1   Neuborne, Ellen. "The Family Business: Who's Next?" *Businessweek*, November 10, 1999. And Ward, John L. *Keeping the Family Business Healthy: How to Plan for Continuing Growth, Profitability, and Family Leadership.* San Francisco: Jossey-Bass Publishers, 1987.

2   The Family Business Institute. "Succession Planning." Accessed on October 29, 2023. https://www.familybusinessinstitute.com/consulting/succession-planning/.

3   Neuborne, Ellen. "The Family Business: Who's Next?" *Businessweek*, November 10, 1999. And Ward, John L. *Keeping the Family Business Healthy: How to Plan for Continuing Growth, Profitability, and Family Leadership.* San Francisco: Jossey-Bass Publishers, 1987.

me remind you: On average, an investment banker will get you 24% *More* money for your company than you'd get if you tried to sell it yourself. *Doesn't it make sense to pay three percent to make twenty-four percent?*

Finally, some company owners may be reluctant to sell at all, out of fear they might be "selling too early." My number one answer is that is: "You don't have to choose the timing perfectly. In fact, the timing will never be perfect."

We can easily structure a deal that gives you value today *and* will give you value over the next three years if the company keeps growing. You can even choose to sell only part of your company if you want some liquidity now or if you want to decrease your involvement and your workload.

So those are some of the benefits of hiring a competent, experienced investment banker the moment you start thinking about selling all or part of your company.

The following chapters will use real-world examples and personal experience to show you why investment bankers are so valuable to company owners. We'll dive into the key roles of a financial advisor and what you can expect from a relationship. We'll also discuss the importance of urgency in deal-making and the real reasons why investment bankers outperform entrepreneurs in deal performance.

Additionally, this book will highlight the best (and some of the most difficult) deals I've made in my career, what I've learned from them, and how they apply to your current situation. We'll explore how to value your company, avoid common mistakes, and navigate negotiations. I'll even take you behind the curtain of M&A deals to show you how it all really happens, offering legal advice, valuation advice, and insight on selecting the right partners in the process.

Each step of the way, we'll focus on building the clarity you need to make informed decisions. Remember, clarity isn't just about having the *right* information, but also about knowing how to use it. It's about understanding your options, your goals, and the realities of the market. With clarity, you can approach the sale of your company without anxiety or uncertainty. Instead, you'll hold confidence and excitement about the future.

I'd be lying if I said it didn't matter if you hired us or not after you read this book. But whatever decision you make about who to work with, I will have succeeded if I've shown you how to think about selling all or part of the company you've worked so long and so hard to develop. So, let's get going on this journey towards clarity. Your future self will thank you for the time and effort you're investing now to make the best possible decision about your company and your future. "Show me the menu and I'll tell you what I want."

CHAPTER 3

HOW INVESTMENT BANKERS GET YOU MORE MONEY, MORE PEACE, AND MORE TIME

If you're reading this book, you're probably looking to sell your company, or perhaps you're a wealth manager or financial advisor working with a client who is contemplating selling their company.

Admittedly, there's romance and bragging rights when doing the deal yourself without the assistance of an individual trained and experienced in the art and science of selling companies. Yes, you'll be able to tell your friends at the country club, "I did the sale all by myself."

But at what cost?

As we've noted, on average, investment bankers win their clients valuations that are twenty-four percent higher than what the company owners could have gotten on their own.

Yes, investment bankers charge a fee, typically two to four percent, but isn't it worth paying that to enjoy that twenty-four percent boost in valuation? Not to mention getting better terms and securing the future role one might desire. Isn't it worth staying focused on running the company during the sale process and being protected from the emotional rollercoaster a sale can involve?

I've worked in investment banking and the financial services industry for over two decades. My Republic Capital Group team and I have helped hundreds of clients reach rewarding, highly lucrative exits. If you're ready to sell your company, I urge you to hire an investment banker instead of trying to sell it on your own. Let me share with you three reasons why.

PROFESSIONAL GUIDANCE IS WORTH MORE THAN MONEY

Let's recap the three advantages you'll gain from an investment banker. It's important to explore each benefit: more money, peace of mind, and time.

MORE MONEY

Investment bankers get you more money by generating more offers. The more offers you have, the more likely someone in the group is highly motivated to acquire your company. The study I mentioned earlier covered 4,468 transactions over two decades and delivered that average valuation premium of twenty-four percent more.

But I want to point out another important figure from that study: Roughly ninety-nine percent of the 1,727 deals completed by *institutional investors* used an investment banker. Simply put, the pros know the value of investment banking, and so should you.

MORE PEACE OF MIND

Over and over, clients have told me how much they enjoyed our management of the process, giving them a sense of control. Most of them have experienced the frustration of chasing lenders or investors—trying to convince someone to work with them.

Our process changes that dynamic, so instead of doing the pursuing, you are being pursued. *Everyone wants to be wanted.* This feeling of control also brings a sense of peace and calm, which is priceless in a stressful world. The sense of peace is widely cited in a 1981 study by S.C. Thompson, called *Will It Hurt Less if I Can Control It? A Complex Answer to a Simple Question.* Thompson's research shows that the perception of control over events and situations dramatically cuts anxiety levels and stress.[1] I've seen first-hand that clients benefit when investment bankers manage a stressful sales process.

---

1   Thompson, S. C. (1981). Will it hurt less if I can control it? A complex answer to a simple question. *Psychological Bulletin, 90*(1), 89–101. https://doi.org/10.1037/0033-2909.90.1.89

MORE TIME FOR YOU

One of the things any good business coach will teach you is: Don't try to be good at the things you don't have any natural ability for. Don't attempt to do important things you haven't been trained to do. Find your unique ability, your superpower, and make the most of it. And then delegate everything else.

One of the main reasons to delegate is the high cost of time spent working on something outside of your core expertise or skill set. The amount of time you will spend working on your transaction without experience is significant. Selling a business could take you 500 hours over eight months. Depending on the number of interested parties and due diligence required, it could take even more time over a longer period.

As a banker, I intuitively understand the many nuances of each step, so I can get deals done faster. Our team creates a financial model and presentation for our clients because it's what we do every day. The alternative is the company owner wasting valuable time and effort figuring it out.

Not only will we be faster, but the work will also be higher quality. Sometimes, when people try to sell their company, their company's performance dips because they are spending so much time away from their leadership role while working to sell the company. They're expending effort that otherwise would have benefited the company.

Potential buyers are apt to notice that the company has been slowing for the last three or four months, and that doesn't look good, does it? When that happens, it usually results in a lower negotiated price at closing. So, here's the irony: you could be working extremely hard to close the deal to sell your company while your company suffers, and you ultimately take home less money at the closing! Doesn't sound like a good strategy, does it?

Instead, imagine having the time to continue running the company while someone else sells it for you. As Warren Buffett said, "I can buy anything I want, but I can't buy time."[1]

DON'T BE FOOLED BY SPREADSHEETS: SELLING IS AN EMOTIONAL GAME

The only certainty in life . . . is uncertainty. We just never know what's coming down the pike. As I mentioned earlier, nobody could have predicted the COVID pandemic or that much of the world would shut down. We also can't predict what will happen in our personal lives. Illness, divorce, losses of loved ones . . . I'm not trying to be negative, I'm being realistic. Unexpected things happen in life.

---

1   Lashbrooke, Barnaby. "Warren Buffett Thinks You Cannot Buy Time, But What If You Could?" *Forbes*, January 24, 2019. https://www.forbes.com/sites/barnabylashbrooke/2019/01/24/warren-buffett-thinks-you-cannot-buy-time-but-what-if-you-could/.

So, here's the challenge: Humans are heavily driven by emotions and not facts.[1] Sometimes, we make suboptimal decisions because we're either afraid of something happening or we're overly optimistic about something happening.

On an emotional level, an outcome with only a five percent likelihood may seem far more likely than an outcome with a thirty percent likelihood. Why do people buy lottery tickets or play slot machines? Because they think they have one chance in two. Either they win or they lose. They don't consider just how unlikely it is to win. So, when you're negotiating what may be the biggest deal of your life, it's important to put the intellect above emotion. A key role for your investment banker is to help you navigate the emotions of a deal. There's been a lot of discussion in recent years about emotional intelligence (EQ). Keeping your emotions in check and thinking logically and calmly is very important. It's also critical to realize that emotions are a core part of who we are as humans. We aren't machines that *feel*; we are *feelers* who think. We are feelers first. Keeping your emotions in check is considerably easier when you have a professional at your side.

---

1   Slovic, Paul, Melissa L. Finucane, Ellen Peters, and Donald G. Mac-Gregor. "The Affect Heuristic." In *Heuristics and Biases: The Psychology of Intuitive Judgment*, edited by Thomas Gilovich, Dale Griffin, and Daniel Kahneman, 397-420. Cambridge University Press, 2002. The authors determine that humans tend to fall back on their feelings and emotions (affect heuristic) when quickly assessing cost-benefit analysis. They commonly ignore facts or analytical reasoning.

Another crucial role your investment banker can play is as a buffer between you and your potential buyer. Your banker can help you discuss sensitive issues without losing your cool and, perhaps much more importantly, without triggering their emotions.

Two of my clients stand out as some of the most logical and numbers-driven people I've ever worked with. One was an engineer, and the other was an accountant. They were both highly accomplished and very intelligent. Engaging with them was both enjoyable and challenging because of the level of intellect each possessed. However, in each case, an issue arose that hit an emotional nerve. No matter how many times I explained or tried to help them see things more clearly, they could not comprehend the full picture because their emotions got involved.

In one case, we had to review simple mathematical calculations three or four times. Each time we discussed the issue, the client returned to his original emotional interpretation of a specific piece of the transaction. So, I'd start over and try to find a different way to help this highly intelligent person understand the facts behind the emotions.

Sellers don't realize that they can be completely unsophisticated about the sales process, or completely unreasonable in their demands. Frankly, both situations scare potential buyers and can kill deals. I've seen strong buyers reject high-quality companies because they grew concerned about the owner's approach and ability to function as a company partner.

This is why it's so important for anyone looking to sell their company to hire a good banker with strong values. I hope it will be us, but if it's someone else, I will have created value for you by sharing with you the sales process. The values that govern Republic Capital Group were instilled in me at an early age, and they shaped my worldview in a way relevant to anyone considering doing business with us. More about this in the next chapter.

CHAPTER 4

MY STORY: FROM MAIN STREET TO WALL STREET

My passion for helping company owners succeed comes from my own journey, from humble beginnings to where I am today.

I grew up in the type of environment you'd hope to find in a minister's home. We were a loving family—loving toward one another, loving toward others, and generous to everyone. My parents wanted to do everything they could to help people and show goodness, and I saw that quality manifest itself in them all the time. Even with limited economic means, they would do things for others in need. They set that example for us from an early age.

THE BLACK JEEP CHEROKEE

One time, my dad was talking to an immigrant pastor serving a poor immigrant community and learned the pastor was walking several miles each day to fulfill his duties and care for his family. On the spot, my dad said, "You are leaving here with this car." The man was in shock and stammered a bit, but my dad would not take no for an answer. He gave the man his own black Jeep Cherokee. I learned later that my father had witnessed his own father do the same thing for someone else. For parents reading this, we should remember that more is caught than is taught. Our kids will model our behavior.

Now for the amazing part. My dad reconnected with the immigrant pastor twenty years later and he was as thankful as ever and still serving others. He was also still driving the black Jeep Cherokee! He meticulously cared for that car and it lasted.

We never know how our generosity will change someone else's life and those around them. My favorite part of the story is that this pastor was still serving the poor. When you have that impulse to do something good and generous, do it! You may be changing the future for many people for years to come.

THE VALUE OF PEOPLE

Growing up, we lived in Louisiana until I turned six. Some of my early memories include going out on the bayou in a little fishing boat with my dad and my brothers. We had catfish traps we would put in the water, baited with awful, pungent cheese that you would never want to smell. But it worked! Eventually, my dad's work led him to move to Augusta, Georgia. Between those two childhood homes—Louisiana and Georgia—I had a real Southern upbringing. A Southern upbringing in our home meant friendliness to all, a slower pace of life that included time for interaction with others, and a strong loyalty to family and friends. We also had the blessing of parents who fully embraced every race. I can remember the Vietnamese, Japanese, and Black pastors my parents befriended, and all the time our family spent with their families and congregations. It was a wonderful way to grow up, just focused on the content of people's character as the great Dr. Martin Luther said in his famous "I Have a Dream" speech. I'm so grateful I was taught to never make assumptions about anyone based on their nationality, skin color, or gender. Our nation's founders said it best: "We hold these truths to be self-evident, that all men are created equal, that they are endowed by their Creator with certain unalienable Rights, that among these are Life, Liberty and the pursuit of Happiness" (The Declaration of Independence—July 4, 1776)

OUTCOME IS SUPERIOR TO PROCESS

We lived in a typical middle-class neighborhood for a few years, but our Georgia home was a new double-wide trailer on a twenty-acre horse farm. My parents planned to build a house up on the main hill of the property. We had seven horses and a mule and with twenty acres as our playground, we weren't inside playing video games. I'm not trying to cast aspersion on kids today; it was just a different experience than most people have now.

My two brothers and I built our own three-hole golf course in the various pastures. There were no greens to speak of, but we all developed good short games by using our irons a lot. Our neighbor was somewhat affluent and had built their own clay tennis court. Their son was really into tennis with coaches, practice, and playing in youth tournaments. I was a basketball player but became his practice dummy, meaning I would play him and lose all of the time, at first. Soon I started learning some strategy and could win more often. It's a funny memory for me because he would get frustrated and call it junk tennis, but I learned two important things. First your opponent is vulnerable when they are convinced they are better than you; even if that is true it doesn't mean they will win that particular game. One reason we love sports is sometimes the team that "can't win" does and that happens in business a lot. The second thing I learned is that sometimes you can use unconventional steps or actions within the accepted process to produce a winning outcome. I hit shots he didn't expect me to because I wasn't getting the same training he was. Outcome is superior to process, meaning that if you win, no one cares about how you did it, and if you lose, you don't get points for your process.

Now before this sounds like I had some kind of unique tennis talent, let's be clear, some of those shots were a desperate attempt to keep the point alive! But I still won more games than I "should" have.

A DEFINING MOMENT OF CHILDHOOD

I still have a vivid memory of something that happened on the farm when I was ten years old.

The horses on our property were gentle quarter horses—horses you ride for pleasure, not high-strung thoroughbreds. But one day, Carrie, my two-year-old sister got behind one of the horses passing through the yard, and our dog suddenly started barking. Looking back now, perhaps the dog was trying to get her to move away, but his barking startled the horse, and it kicked out and hit Carrie right in the stomach.

My mom, just a few feet away, didn't see it happen, but she heard her cry out. She ran over to Carrie, who was on the ground, crying and clutching her belly. My mom pulled up Carrie's shirt, and she could see the hoof print, so she knew for sure what had just happened. By the time they got to the hospital, however, the hoof print had faded, and the medical staff began to question my mom. They didn't want to do much for Carrie because they couldn't find anything wrong with her. She wasn't showing any evidence of a medical problem at that point.

Fortunately, my parents knew a doctor at another hospital who had performed surgery on me when I had appendicitis. So, they said, "We want to be discharged. We are going over to St. Joseph's to see another doctor." They knew that while expert advice is to be highly valued, sometimes having firsthand knowledge and insight can trump data and years of experience. It's crucial to understand these moments in business. I've seen a company's value diminished by following accepted business wisdom that was counterproductive based on the specific situation. A good investment banker can help greatly with this dynamic; the exceptions to accepted ideas can lead to exceptional outcomes.

When the next doctor heard the story, he listened to her stomach through his stethoscope and said, "I don't like this. I agree with you; something isn't right." Sure enough, when they took an X-ray, they saw an air bubble forming. The impact had punctured her intestine, which is a potentially fatal injury that can trigger sepsis. They immediately rushed my two-year-old sister into surgery. She was brought in, cleaned, and stitched up internally, and afterward, she never had any further symptoms or issues. She made a full recovery.

Today, reflecting on that incident, I see it as an example of parents who didn't have wealth but had a lot of intelligence and knew when to use their social skills and connections. They knew that firsthand knowledge sometimes trumps "the experts" and to hold fast in those situations. This has served me well many times in deals when the experts felt something could not be achieved, but we had a plan and strategy based on information and insight that led to success. My parents were willing to do whatever it took to protect their children. If you're a parent, I'm sure you feel the same way.

GROWING UP IN OHIO

When I was twelve, we moved to Northwest Ohio between Toledo and Cleveland, again because of my father's work. We ended up in a little farming town, far from the Deep South—a fact that was brought home the first time I spoke up in class. Everyone turned toward me when they heard my accent. I immediately decided I would lose that Southern accent as quickly as I could.

I had a fairly positive high school experience. I played basketball and that was my outlet and filled my free time. I had the experience of some success and adversity playing for high school teams. Part of my growing experience was when my family moved to another school district for my senior year. Being the new kid as a senior was another chance to forge new friendships and develop my social skills. My school experience of moving from the South to the Midwest helped me go from a shy ninth grader to a confident young man who could easily meet strangers and make new friends wherever I went.

By the time I graduated from high school, I had gotten pretty involved in my church and volunteered as the youth director. Then, I had a chance to join a unique kind of Bible school in Texas that was very hands-on and focused on serving the less fortunate.

We would travel to Beaumont, Texas, which I was told at that time had the highest per-capita number of gang members in the country. We would go into gated apartment complexes surrounded by barbed wire. We had a big box trailer, painted hot pink with a dinosaur on it. The side of it would pull down and become a stage where we would put on a kid's program. We served food and had a drawing for one boy's bike and one girl's bike. I have a vivid memory of learning about the impact of marketing. Coke was always the top choice of drink, until the week a new Grant Hill commercial came out for Sprite. Hill was a famous NBA player, and that Saturday, Sprite was most requested drink. A couple of kids even said, "Give me some Sprite like Grant Hill." More importantly, I learned the joy and impact that investing in young people can have on your own life.

In 1991, Russia opened to Westerners for the first time. In 1993 I was part of a team that went over to Russia to work with young people. For six months, I lived in a Russian city of nearly three million people, about 400 miles northeast of Moscow. Living so far away from home, in such a different type of society, helped me understand people in ways I could not have if I had stayed stateside. I gained the perspective that since the US is only six percent of the world's population, in some ways it's only six percent of reality. In addition, it showed me the difference between a society that respects faith and a society that rejects it.

THE PASTORAL LIFE

After completing that program and returning home, I got married, got a job in financial services, and started living my adult life. I was a financial advisor for the first five years of my career, and enjoyed the process of meeting with clients and saying, "What are your goals?" and "Let's make and execute a plan to help you." I was successful at this and won many awards as I rapidly moved up the company ladder.

At that time, my father was the pastor of a church in Ohio, but he was also active in serving the poor in the Philippines by developing programs to feed children. At one point, they were feeding 3,000 children a day through child development centers. After making these trips for over ten years, my father believed he should devote all his time to this effort. So, there was a discussion among the church leadership, who decided to offer me the opportunity to take over as the senior pastor of the church. I accepted and left financial services to become a full-time clergyman.

After a few years of ministry, a door opened that was beyond anything I had imagined. While attending a conference in another state, I connected with a large and thriving church community. Not long after, I received a call that would change the course of my life. A church across the country wanted me to come lead their youth ministry. But this wasn't just any church. They recently completed a massive expansion and moved their sanctuary from a 1,300-seat auditorium to a brand new 5,000-seat auditorium. For lack of a better word, it was a megachurch—and they were looking for someone to take over the 1,300-seat facility and fill it with the next generation. They believed I was that person. After a season of prayer and reflection, I knew this was the next step God was calling me to take. So, I packed up everything, moved across the country, and not long after settling into our new town, we welcomed our first child into the world.

I have learned over the years that you can correctly choose your next steps in life, but that doesn't mean things will work out the way you think. It's a common mistake to assume the initial outcome of a decision is its only metric. Many accomplished business leaders attribute much of their success to things that didn't work out. To this day, I haven't doubted my decision. In fact, I think it was part of the learning path that brought me back to working in the financial services field. Ultimately, the church had some significant internal turmoil that I was not a part of. Because of the unsettled nature of things, it was necessary to move on.

LIFE IN THE SUNSHINE STATE

After some time reflecting and considering my options, I decided to go to Florida to work for a business with my brother doing real estate lending. The company was doing well during a nationwide lending boom. My brother and I trained and managed the salespeople, and we got pretty good at it. I went from making a young minister's salary to earning five times that. Our teams led production for the entire company and things were running smoothly. However, our boss was young and inexperienced and, one day, he got aggressive with my brother and tried to impose a strategy that my brother considered terrible for his team. He wanted us to completely change our approach, which was already successful and lucrative for all involved—including our boss! An experienced manager would never do something like this without at least some dialogue with those he was leading. My brother objected to the immediate implementation of the strategy, and our boss fired him on the spot. He then marched into my office and said, "Langston, I just fired your brother. I need to know if you're in or you're out." I paused for a moment, then said, "Well, my brother brought me on, so I guess I'm out."

Another layer to the story is that my brother and I had hired and trained our younger brother Daniel, and he was doing well. It was a good job for him, and he was skilled at it. But when we walked out, Daniel joined us. The boss had inadvertently lost three of his top people in one stroke! The lesson was clear to me: If you have a successful strategy, don't mess with it, and don't alienate the people who work hard for you.

My decision to leave that day was the first step of my entrepreneurial journey. My brother and I started a new company, entirely on our own. We had no partners. Then we started another business. Eventually, we had three companies, all built around lending, titling, and brokering real estate transactions. During this time, I decided to finish my education to better myself, so I went back to school and got my MBA at Rollins College in Winter Park, Florida.

After graduating in 2007, I came to realize that my highest and best use of my skills and interests would be to return to the world of financial services and investment management to work at the intersection of numbers and people. I also looked around at the real estate market and thought, *Boy, this may not be headed in a good direction.* I realized I needed to sell all my companies, but wanted to make sure our employees had a good opportunity with a new firm.

My instincts were correct—the real estate market was about to crash.

As a result, I did my first M&A deal. I connected with the owners of a large mortgage and real estate company with over one hundred loan officers and one hundred real estate agents. They were the largest in the Southeast, and I persuaded them to acquire us. Although it was an all-equity transaction and I knew the value of that equity in the future was in question, it gave my entire team roles in a leading company, and I was able to execute the deal quickly to pursue my new path.

ENTERING A DARK TIME . . . AND COMING OUT OF IT

When the real estate market crashed in 2008, it triggered the Great Recession. My income went down seventy percent, and my real estate assets were down sixty-five percent.

I was millions of dollars in debt and couldn't make any money for most of 2008. I didn't see any way out. As I looked at my kids, I thought about the Bible verse, "God will not visit the sins of the father unto the children." I prayed that it was true and that my kids would fair better than me, but I felt terrible about myself and worried about my kids. I felt I had failed them.

In 2009, I made the tough decision to file for

bankruptcy so that I wouldn't be locked into years of trying to repay debts and being unable to provide for my children—who were between the ages of three and six.

I moved from a gated community to an apartment. My power was turned off at one point because I owed the electric company $1,200. I can remember standing on the street corner outside my office, thinking about who to call. I just needed $1,200. It sounds like such a small amount of money now, but at that moment, it was a lot. I had lunch at the time with a successful executive and investor, and he told me something that transformed my thinking to this day. He said, "No one has a plan for losing seventy percent of their income and assets. This was a historic real estate collapse and sometimes the market just moves against you, and you can't blame yourself for that."

He went on to tell me that during the dot-com boom of the late 1990s, he had multi-million-dollar paper profits on one of the high-flying companies that were household names back then. He refused to sell when he should have, and instead he lost those millions of dollars of profits because he was hoping for even more. "That was just stupid," he said of his actions. "What happened to you is just life. The best thing you can do is forget it and go on and become successful." (*Thank you, Nathan, for your encouragement, you made a significant impact on me at a time when I was very low.*)

Fortunately, I landed a role at the most significant firm in my region in financial services that was raising capital for private investments and working with wealthy clients and financial advisors. I was able to land that role by waiting on a bench in the walkway that was located between the office tower where the company was and the parking garage. I had met the president of the company networking several weeks earlier, but he wasn't replying to my emails, and I had no other direct connection to him. When he approached on his walk to the parking garage from the building, I stood up and said, "Hello Jeff," and he responded warmly. It turns out all my emails had gone to his spam, at a time before there were more sophisticated filters. Three weeks later I was in the role and had a great two-year run of growth and leading my division in business growth.

Sometimes you have be willing to try unconventional things to get results. I knew this was the only firm I could join to meet the goals I had for my career and so when the idea came to me to go down to the company headquarters in person, I did. I was actually sitting on the bench when it fully dawned on me that I was in the perfect spot because no one could leave the building without passing me. Risk taking is often cited as a key to success, but I would encourage you to realize that many times it means taking a personal ego risk. Sometimes you have to risk being embarrassed or falling flat on your face to succeed. Many people spend capital to build a business like it will never run out but won't take these personal ego risks.

For my next assignment I was given a great opportunity to join a private investment firm in Houston. It was my first chance to work with a firm that was part of the portfolio of a global private equity firm. Private equity firms of this size are at the pinnacle of private investments and mergers and acquisitions of private companies. The firm was Summit Partners, a Boston-based firm. As part of the leadership team, I saw firsthand how professional investors determined a company's value and how they interacted with buyers and sellers. It was very valuable experience.

I continued to grow professionally and next joined a prestigious firm based in New York City. I finally arrived on Wall Street! Well, sort of—I still lived in Houston. But it was a great opportunity with a firm that was leading its category with some really talented people. It's always great to be with a winning organization. I learned a lot about how some New York City firms see the world. It was an invaluable experience because I also saw how fear and anxiety can play a powerful role in a company.

Today, my wife and I spend a good amount of time in New York. We own an apartment there and we love it. That said I found myself in a situation where New York City was a lot further from Houston than the 1,410 miles that separated them. So, I found myself looking for a new role and joined a Houston financial firm backed by the Carlyle Group, the second largest private equity firm in the world at the time. The experience of working with them and learning from them was invaluable. This experience of working with world-class investors prepared me for the next phase of my purpose in life and business.

THE BIRTH OF REPUBLIC CAPITAL GROUP

Eventually, I saw the opportunity to launch Republic Capital Group, which led me on my own entrepreneurial journey. Today nine years later, I'm fortunate that the firm is incredibly successful—but I've had a lot of help.

People have given me opportunities, and I've tried to make the most of them. I've overcome hard times and come out the other side better and stronger for what I went through. This helps me understand and empathize with company owners whose careers have not gone up in a straight line—which is pretty much everybody! And that's also why I like to remind others that we all need help sometimes.

Conviction always underlies my interactions with company owners who are reluctant to reach out to Republic Capital Group for the help they need. That understanding comes from my upbringing and the highs and lows I've experienced.

LANGSTON WEALTH MANAGEMENT CENTER AT THE UNIVERSITY OF TEXAS, MCCOMBS SCHOOL OF BUSINESS

In 2021, I met Dr. Ramesh Rao, the McDermott Professor of Finance and Director of the McCombs Wealth Management Initiative at the University of Texas. We met for breakfast tacos in Austin as any good Texans would. I was excited to talk more about the Wealth Management Center he recently launched at the McCombs School of Business. It was unique to have a center like this as part of a prestigious business school at the fifth largest university in the United States. I was determined and passionate about helping students and giving back to the industry. We had talked before and had been comparing notes for several weeks by phone, but this was our first in-person meeting. After some discussion, he declared that I should endow and name the wealth management center. I was flattered and tried not to laugh but said, "Look, I'm a young man and still growing my company. Let's set our sights a bit lower." After the meeting, I had an idea that the best way to help would be to set up a fellowship to provide scholarships for high performing students who elected to take wealth management as their minor. So, I called my wife fully expecting her to save me from my idea. You see Candace and I are a blended family. I brought four kids to the marriage, and she brought four kids as well! Yes, we have eight kids between us, and no, most people can't believe it either. When I called her, I was thinking she was probably going to say, "Honey remember we have our own kids to put through college," however, when I shared the idea of the fellowship and how we could impact young people she said, "I love this idea!" and the Langston Fellowship was born! (Baby number nine!)

Today there are over forty Langston Fellows, and we are so proud to be supporting such talented and diligent young people from all over the world who have come to study at McCombs.

In 2024, I did my own transaction at Republic, bringing on a strategic partner to help us grow. Merchant Investment Management is a leading investor in our space backed by Sixth Street Capital, one of the premier private equity firms in the US and one of only a handful authorized to invest in the NFL. This put us in the position to have the incredible honor and opportunity to officially endow the Langston Wealth Management Center. For a kid who grew up on twenty acres in a double wide trailer, it was the ultimate "turtle on a fencepost" moment. We are so excited to be part of the next generation of wealth management leaders and help shape the future of the industry.

Candace and I believe wealth is having the time, health, and resources to accomplish the purpose you were born for. We believe your purpose involves your strengths and is for the betterment of others. We hope to instill in the students a drive to serve others and leverage wealth for good.

Now that I've shared something about who I am, let me explain in greater detail exactly what investment bankers do and how we can help you. I'll also help contrast different professionals and how you should evaluate choosing between them. There's a reason the most successful deals in history had investment bankers guiding them every step of the way and you should too.

CHAPTER 5

INVESTMENT BANKERS VERSUS BUSINESS BROKERS

In this chapter, we'll explore the differences between investment bankers and business brokers. No disrespect intended to business brokers, but if your company is worth a lot of money, going with an investment banker who specializes in M&A is the wise choice.

An investment banker is an advisor—a financial, emotional, mental, and occasionally even a spiritual advisor.

For company owners, investment banking deals are the most important financial events in their entire lives. They can raise capital, sell a company, or make a significant acquisition to take the company to the next level.

The best investment bankers know how interconnected market events and trends are. They understand that success comes from weaving all these elements together. We know when to focus our attention on the financial aspect of a transaction and when to empha-size the emotional side.

Investment bankers orchestrate a symphony that produces the outcome their clients want. They do everything they can within legal and ethical limits to help their clients accomplish their goals.

Investment bankers are not business brokers. I will explain all the qualifications an investment banker must obtain, while a business broker can normally operate with a real estate brokerage license or no license at all. We help identify risks in transac-tions. We are involved in raising capital, working on restructuring compensation plans, and/or guiding a sale. Our ability to provide enterprise-level thinking separates us from others in our field.

QUALIFICATIONS AND TRAINING

One key credential that sets leading investment bankers apart from other advisors is their specific licensing obtained through the SEC or FINRA. We are required to pass a number of rigorous multi-hour examinations. These tests require meaningful study and an understanding of company transactions, the laws governing them, tax issues, and other aspects of business. The licensing exams qualify and quan-tify the knowledge a person must have mastered to become an investment banker.

There are also stringent regulations regarding a

licensed investment banker's criminal and financial history. You must be fingerprinted, and the FBI will conduct a background check using your fingerprints to ensure that you have not been involved in any illegal activity.

So, a licensed investment banker has passed a government background check regarding any illegal activity and financial activity. Many investment bankers have undergraduate degrees in business and finance, and many have MBAs. By contrast, most business brokers do not have this kind of rigorous training, education, or oversight. That's quite a difference in the professional level of who will be leading this crucial transaction for you.

As an entrepreneur, I am familiar with the notion that degrees and licenses are no guarantee of success. I have met many successful business people who have achieved success without having a master's degree. I've also had clients who didn't graduate from high school yet built multiple successful financial firms worth hundreds of millions of dollars. As an entrepreneur, however, I felt the need to go back and learn more. My MBA has been invaluable for me. It helped me understand how to learn quickly, where to find information, and how to fill in the blanks and connect the dots. My MBA studies enhanced my entrepreneurial skills and made my investment banking work significantly more effective.

THE CORE QUALITIES OF A GREAT INVESTMENT BANKER

When you're ready to sell your company, you need more than just another advisor. You need a partner who's been in the trenches. You need someone who brings real expertise to your corner. That's why investment bankers need intensive technical training.

Experienced investment bankers know how to model financials and value companies properly. We've spent decades learning the specific things that help you increase your company's value and get higher bids. Ours is battle-tested expertise that protects your interests, not just theoretical knowledge.

The best bankers also thrive on complexity. Great deals succeed when bankers see opportunities where others see challenges. Great investment bankers turn complexity into opportunity, boosting final deals by that twenty-four percent premium we've discussed.

You also need someone who won't give up when things get tough. Later on, I'll discuss an extremely complex deal featuring five parties, five legal teams, and a six-month deadline. These types of transactions test one's resolve. A great investment banker will push through challenges to achieve a deal.

Being honest while telling your company's story in a compelling way is another crucial skill. We've learned how to present your value in a way that resonates with buyers while maintaining integrity.

Finally, you need someone who can orchestrate all the moving parts. Getting deals done isn't just about numbers; it's about coordinating lawyers, accountants, buyers, and sellers and helping everyone keep a cool head when things get emotional. Good deal-making involves anticipating problems before they arise and keeping everything on track until the final payment hits your account. These aren't just checkboxes on a list—they're skills and qualities we've developed through years of successful deal making.

BREADTH OF SERVICES

There's one more thing I want to emphasize about what makes an excellent investment banker: the wide range of services they can provide. In my view, this makes them the most qualified, most vetted option to help you with your deal.

Investment bankers themselves cannot offer legal or tax advice. As a result, our team includes CPAs and J.D.s to assist in determining your best strategy. Additionally, we can help you select outside advisors with specific industry experience related to your company transactions.

Often, company owners who've interviewed various business brokers to advise them on a company transaction will ask me, "What exactly will you help me with?" I've learned that many business brokerage firms say, "You know, we'll do these three things, but you've got to do all of these other things." That's because they're not investment bankers. They aren't licensed. Business brokers have a role to play in the market for sure, but if your company has a meaningful valuation, you'll need more than they can offer.

There are activities in which business brokers can't participate because they aren't licensed to handle those responsibilities. Those activities matter greatly and separate the investment-bank-led deal, which contributes that twenty-four percent sale premium, from the deal the seller handles himself or herself.

The truth is that the work of selling a business is time-consuming. For example, you must decide on timing, what percentage to sell, and whether you want to stay involved. You also need to understand your future role with the buyer (if any) and make many other significant decisions.

But how are you supposed to make these decisions if you've never made them before?

What parameters should you apply?

What's the difference between selling thirty percent of a business and sixty percent?

How do you set a price for the business?

How much do you negotiate from that number, when, and how?

If you're drowning in these questions, the good news is that Republic Capital Group is a full-service investment banking firm. We will assist and support you in every aspect of the transaction, helping you navigate your questions and reach sound conclusions.

Again, of course, we won't be able to give legal advice—you will certainly need outside counsel for legal or tax advice. However, we can assist in locating qualified professionals and coordinate with them all the time and we have our own general counsel to help consult with your counsel.

But the bottom line is that a strong, confident investment banker and investment banking firm will be with you every step of the way, from the idea's inception until the funds have been sent and cleared into your account. Many times, we will continue working with you after that, wrapping up any necessary details.

Don't fall into the trap of listening to people who say, "Yes, I advise on transactions." What does that *really* mean? Maybe they've worked on a few deals, and that's why sellers must understand the difference between an investment banker and a company broker. Most importantly, you'll want to recognize that this difference pertains to training, experience, and skill, which could mean millions of dollars more in your outcome. Even more importantly, don't fall into the trap of going it alone.

At Republic Capital Group, we mitigate challenges before they arise and manage every detail carefully. We don't just identify risks; we offer solutions. Our goal is to be a true partner, not just during the deal but also through every stage of the process, ensuring you achieve the best possible results for your company.

Remember, the difference between a good investment banker and a great one can mean millions of dollars in your pocket. It represents peace of mind, knowing that your life's work is in the best possible hands. Don't settle for less when it comes to your legacy!

So now you know what investment bankers do and what separates us from business brokers. If the benefits we provide are appealing enough, you might be wondering when to make the crucial move of engaging an investment advisor. Let's explore the question of timing in the next chapter.

CHAPTER 6

WHEN SHOULD I HIRE AN INVESTMENT BANKER?

If your instincts say it might be time to raise capital, buy a company, or sell your company, contact an investment banker now! *Trust your instincts.* In my experience, the instincts of successful company owners are often spot-on. The preparation necessary to maximize your outcome doesn't happen overnight, so get started immediately. The sooner we start, the more flexibility you'll have regarding timing, strategy, and execution.

As I noted in a previous chapter, one of the things you don't have a lot of is time and it's the one thing you can't buy. That's what Warren Buffett said, and if it's true for him, it's certainly true for the rest of us! Not acting now could end up costing you plenty of time, money, and opportunity costs. Let's explore all these factors.

TIME KILLS DEALS

Waiting too long can be costly. Staying too long at the party can mean you risk losing your welcome. Life is unpredictable, and anything can happen— tomorrow or the day after. Even the most successful companies can face challenges that can derail the best-laid plans.

In the world of company transactions, momentum is everything. When you're ready to sell or raise capital, every day that passes becomes a day when market conditions could change, competitors could emerge, or your company could face unexpected challenges.

For example, regulatory environments can shift without warning, and technology can change the game overnight. In 2005, the home video rental giant Blockbuster Video was still dominant. But the streaming technology of Netflix changed everything. Blockbuster had the opportunity to buy Netflix when the new challenger was still in its infancy. Blockbuster passed on the deal and soon went out of business altogether.

Research In Motion or RIM, the maker of Blackberry, the precursor to the iPhone, had the chance to put telephone service into its devices. Its leadership team told its engineers that "Nobody wants a phone on a Blackberry." The iPhone came along and suddenly the Blackberry (nicknamed the "Crackberry" because of its addictive qualities) was history. The stories of once-mighty companies that suddenly disappeared or are just a shadow of their former selves—Kodak, Bethlehem Steel, and Circuit City come to mind—all too familiar.

Your company likely has a positive story right now—growth, profitability, market leadership. This narrative is what attracts buyers and investors but business cycles are real, and what goes up often comes down.

A CHALLENGE IN YOUR COMPANY CAN SET YOU BACK YEARS

I had a client who ran an incredibly successful company. It was one of the fastest-growing firms in his industry anywhere in the United States. We went to the marketplace, found an outstanding buyer, and received a letter of intent agreeing to the initial terms of the deal.

Everything was on track, but then the owner got a letter in the mail: "You are being sued." Everything suddenly stopped. He battled the lawsuit for three and a half long years. Though ultimately cleared of any wrongdoing, it took him nearly four and a half years to sell his company.

Lawsuits can hit anyone, anytime. While some investors might overlook legal challenges, most prefer to avoid uncertainty. If my client had started the sale process just a few months earlier, none of that delay and unhappiness would have occurred. That's why timing is so crucial. It's not just about finding the right buyer or getting the right price; it's about navigating a landscape that can change in an instant.

Lawsuits aren't the only events that change things. Interest rates, supply chain issues, strikes, wars, pandemics, etc. We live in crazy times where the only certainty is uncertainty. Obviously, you can't predict or prepare for the unknown. But you want to be cognizant that the landscape today could shift in a heartbeat.

NO ONE HAS MORE CLARITY ABOUT YOUR COMPANY THAN YOU DO

Right now, you have the clearest picture of your company's performance over the past year. You know your financials, your market position, and your growth trajectory. This clarity is invaluable when presenting your company to potential buyers or investors. Even in the best circumstances, selling a company or raising capital is a complex process that often takes longer than anticipated. There are due diligence periods, negotiations, legal reviews, and more. But by starting now, you give yourself a buffer for these unexpected delays. Your instincts got you this far—trust them again, and don't wait until it's too late to make your move.

Throughout this book, I've emphasized that

having an experienced investment banker by your side can increase your sale price by twenty-four percent or more. In the next chapter, I'll show exactly why that's true.

CHAPTER 7
MANAGING DEAL FATIGUE

As we explored previously, selling a company is more than a financial transaction. It's an emotional one, too. An experienced investment banker understands the psychology of buyers and knows how to build their emotional investment in the deal. Once they're strongly engaged, we can work on enhancing the perceived and actual value of your company in their eyes.

Buyers and investors consider several deal opportunities before choosing one. As a result, it's best to remain emotionally detached until they determine the investment, or purchase, might make sense for them. It's hard to do when there's a lot of money on the table. The emotions surrounding a deal can be exhausting.

Deal fatigue is the terminology used to convey emotional fatigue or exhaustion in transactions. This is a well-known factor in the world of buying and selling transactions. Let's take a moment to define deal fatigue and then see how you can avoid it as you go through your transaction.

The Mayo Clinic describes emotional exhaustion and its connection to stress this way: "When stress from adverse or challenging events in life occur continually, you can find yourself in a state of feeling emotionally worn out and drained. This is called emotional exhaustion. For most people, emotional exhaustion tends to build up slowly over time. Emotional exhaustion includes emotional, physical and performance symptoms."[1]

You can address emotional exhaustion by recognizing the stressors you're able to minimize or eliminate. When you're unable to change a stressor because it's out of your control, it's crucial to focus on the present moment. In the present, many neutral or positive events are occurring. Chances are, nothing bad is happening in the present! As Mark Twain said, "I've had a lot of worries in my life, most of which never happened." When you focus on the neutral or positive events happening in the present moment, you gain perspective. This allows you to shift your focus away from the stressors.

Two things jump out at me from the Mayo Clinic's definition of emotional exhaustion:

---

1   https://www.mayoclinichealthsystem.org/hometown-health/speaking -of-health/emotional-exhaustion-during-times-of-unrest

1. *Reduce any stressors you can control.* The key to a professional transaction process led by an investment banker is that it specifically minimizes many transaction stressors for the seller. These include interactions with multiple buyers or investors; managing their information requests and screening out those buyers or investors who aren't suitable for the seller's goals.

Having an investment banker to handle negotiations in close coordination greatly reduces the seller's stress. Finally, the investment banker helps by managing the relationships with legal and tax counsel.

2. *Regarding things out of your control, focus on the present.* I constantly encourage clients to stay focused on the present, since the future is one of the hardest things to predict! I remind sellers that when we get to a given moment in the future, we will have the information we need to make the best possible decision. We won't have to speculate or guess—we will know what to do.

I refer to this as building brick by brick. It sounds simple, but if each brick is placed correctly and mortared well, you end up with a strong wall. Most anxiety about the future comes from not knowing what's going to happen. If you focus on constantly clarifying everything in the present, as you move forward, the picture will become clearer and clearer. Also remember that you aren't committed until after closing—it isn't over until the ink is dry on the selling documents. You won't close until you enjoy considerable clarity about all aspects of the deal. So, take a deep breath and exhale!

Now, knowing deal fatigue exists and understanding how to manage and mitigate it are two different things. Most people assume that deal fatigue is primarily due to the amount of time the transaction is taking. For example, a six-month transaction process is more likely to lead to deal fatigue as opposed to a three-month process.

This is a corollary of another well-known factor, one that I touched on earlier—the idea that time kills all deals. I like to say that in reality, time *changes* all deals. Some deals simply take longer to close. So, the length of time a deal takes to close is not always the sole source of deal fatigue.

Many people don't understand that deal fatigue is largely driven by the extreme ranges of emotion that can arise, particularly in a disorganized or poorly communicated process. Let's say the seller believes that he has negotiated, at a high level, a deal that he's very excited about. And then something seems to go terribly wrong. Maybe the seller doesn't understand the sales process. Or perhaps there's miscommunication with the buyer as the legal terms emerge when the documents become much more detailed. The seller then grows confused, frustrated, and anxious, because he fears that the deal he was so excited about is changing or falling apart.

These extreme mood swings can lead to emotional problems.[1] In our case, they can cause deal fatigue, in which the seller abandons hope that a deal will ever be made and walks away from what likely would have been a life-changing and highly lucrative exit.

Yes, things should not take too long. But the true antidote to deal fatigue is a clear, consistent process. Ideally, the process should give both sellers *and* buyers a stronger sense of control and understanding of what is happening and what to expect next.

It's also important to work with an investment banking firm that understands that pricing too high or pricing too low is a poor strategy.

Early in my career at my first real financial services company, my boss Bruce shared with me a great insight I've held on to for over twenty years.

I had just lost a large prospect who rejected my proposal, and I was feeling quite down. I worked hard to win this client. It was very disappointing. Bruce said to me, "John, you should always remember that things are never as bad as they seem, nor are they ever as good as they seem. You should always strive to maintain more of an even keel in your emotions and avoid moving to either extreme."

This has been great business advice for me over the years and has been the key to closing some very complicated and highly stressful transactions.

---

1   https://www.medicalnewstoday.com/articles/mood-swings

Maintaining a sense of calm when things are going extremely well and maintaining a sense of calm when things are challenging are the hallmarks of an emotionally intelligent deal maker.

Whoever's managing your transaction should be helping you to manage your emotions, too. You shouldn't be left all alone to deal with the emotional side of selling your business. Having a clear, consistent process, and taking each obstacle or issue as it comes, almost inevitably leads to closing a great deal and taking a big step toward your next adventure!

.

CHAPTER 8
HOW YOU GET THAT
24% MORE

A company owner came to me with an offer of seventy million dollars for one hundred percent of his company. I told him not to accept the offer, even though the number was eye-watering to this gentleman. I explained that the buyer making the offer didn't have the capability to unlock all of the value the company contained. I did some analysis with my team and told my client I believed it would bring a value of $100 million. He said, "If you can get it to $110 million, I'll kiss you!"

Ultimately, I helped him sell the company for $106 million, not just twenty-four percent more but actually fifty percent more than what he was prepared to accept when we first met. I was thrilled to get him that number. I was even happier that we hadn't crossed the $110 million mark—the only person who can kiss me is my wife!

In this chapter, I'll demonstrate why the 24% *More*

title of this book isn't some kind of marketing hook but it's the reality for company owners who use investment bankers.

Yes, investment bankers take the load off your shoulders when you're selling all or part of your company. Yes, we allow you to stay focused on the all-important task of running your company during the sale process, so your sales won't dip and negatively impact your value. And yes, we know the nuances of these transactions, and we can protect you from legal, financial, and emotional pitfalls along the way.

But the best reason for hiring an investment banker to handle a sale of a company is the opportunity for a twenty-four percent higher valuation. In this chapter, we'll run the numbers to demonstrate why that's factual and not just hype.

PROFESSIONAL PROMOTION BEATS SELF PROMOTION ALL DAY, EVERY DAY!

Highly successful company owners, whether they started their company, expanded a preexistent family company, or grew a company they bought, tend to be hands-on kind of people.

Okay, I'm low-key saying that they can be control freaks. Which does come in handy as a business owner. Their success usually comes from deep knowledge and control of everything in the company, from product lines to manufacturing processes to sales. They know what's happening, minute by minute, in their company.

Above all, they know their numbers. Sounds great, right? Yes, however that kind of hands-on control can come back to bite them when they're selling, as can the tendency to let emotions or personalities overrule the intellect.

Part of my role as an investment banker is to earn a high level of trust from my clients. It has to be so high that they're comfortable taking their hands off the steering wheel and letting someone else drive!

Let's discuss why it's so important for the company owner to step back and let the investment banker drive the process all the way to that desired *24% More* outcome.

You'll be far more likely to get the result you want—the highest valuation, the best terms—if you leave the process to the people who have done it countless times for other companies.

Investment bankers bring a structured, methodical approach to selling a company. At Republic Capital Group, we've refined our processes through countless transactions. We ensure that every step, from the first contact to the final talks, is done with precision and expertise. I'll take you through our 14-point process later in the book. This disciplined approach minimizes errors, reduces delays, and improves outcomes.

One of our unique strengths is the ability to adjust

and recalibrate our process based on the needs of a specific company or circumstances that may arise. This has led to a high rate of successful closings and lucrative transactions.

MORE REASONS TO WORK WITH AN INVESTMENT BANKER

When you engage an investment banker, it sends a clear signal to potential buyers that you're serious about the transaction. Buyers know they're dealing with professionals who understand the intricacies of deal-making. This credibility can lead to more serious offers and less time wasted on tire-kickers.

In addition, investment bankers have extensive networks and databases of potential buyers. We know how to craft compelling teasers and confidential information memorandums that attract interest. More importantly, we know how to get these materials in front of the right people. The result? More offers on the table, which often translates to better terms for you.

When buyers know they're competing against other serious offers, they're motivated to put their best foot forward. Investment bankers know how to create this competitive dynamic, often resulting in buyers increasing their bids or improving other terms of the deal.

YOUR FINANCIAL PICTURE IS OPTIMIZED WITH OUR MODELING

Financial modeling is a crucial part of presenting your company. We don't just regurgitate your financial statements; we create sophisticated models that highlight your company's financial potential. This might include adjusting for one-time expenses, highlighting growth trends, or demonstrating the impact of synergies for strategic buyers.

WE CAN SELL YOUR COMPANY'S STRONG MERITS WITHOUT TURNING OFF BUYERS

There's an art to presenting a company's strengths without coming across as boastful or unrealistic. Investment bankers know how to walk this fine line. We can emphasize your company's unique value proposition and competitive advantages in a way that resonates with buyers without raising red flags.

Let's take a look now at things from a buyer's point of view. An effective investment banking process builds momentum toward the goal of emotional stability, excitement, and connection. A solid process delivers information in a professional format. It fosters a professional relationship between the buyer or investor and the company owners.

Once an emotional connection happens, the buyer begins to think a transaction is possible. At that time,

95

it's then appropriate to manage more challenging or negotiable points. Before this momentum builds, you lack the engagement to secure commitments on some deal matters. This is one of the most nuanced parts of a transaction process. It doesn't matter if it's an investment or a sale.

Company owners have so much at stake, it's hard to gauge the buyer's or investor's emotions. This can lead to mismatched communication and objectives between the parties.

The buyer or investor seeks to understand the company. They want to believe a deal could make sense and actually occur. Buyers or investors may have ample capital, but they want to protect their time. They only want to get involved with a seller whose company is a good fit.

A buyer or investor must complete steps and goals in our process. Completing these creates a sense of progression both intellectually and emotionally. As your representative, we communicate efficiently and thoroughly with potential buyers and investors. We clarify things and, yes, we position you and your positive traits in a professional way.

We give buyers feedback about how they stand out from others. We also inform them that we are eliminating some buyers and investors. We must be professional, not just flattering. We will point out areas where we feel that the buyer is a strong, attractive potential buyer or investor.

This communication must be genuine without any gamesmanship. This approach must be part of the culture of the investment bank you work with. Otherwise, the banker is just peddling hype, and that usually leads to disappointment.

WE SEE WAYS TO RESTRUCTURE YOUR COMPANY IN THE TRANSACTION TO INCREASE ITS VALUE SIGNIFICANTLY

Sometimes, small changes in the way your company is structured can have a substantial impact on its value to buyers. We might find ways to improve your company's appeal to buyers. These could include spinning off non-core assets, restructuring debt, or realigning your management team.

Also, an investment banker's most powerful tool is the ability to present your financials in the best light possible. This often involves calculating an adjusted EBITDA, which stands for Earnings Before Interest, Taxes, Depreciation, and Amortization. The goal is to better reflect your company's true earning power.

We know how to find and measure changes that can boost your EBITDA. These might include changes to owner pay, one-time costs, or synergies a strategic buyer could realize. A small increase in adjusted EBITDA can mean millions in added value when applied to the valuation multiple. That factor alone can be a big step forward to the promise of 24% *More*!

THE VALUE OF LETTING GO

A key to a successful sale is knowing when to step back and let experts take over. Investment bankers bring experience, networks, and negotiation skills from many deals. Company owners often find selling their company tougher than expected. They face challenges throughout the entire process, from creating a story to talking with buyers.

As we've seen, a seller's emotions can hinder a sale. This isn't surprising because your company is your creation! You dreamed it, built it, and devoted much of your life to its success. How could you not be emotional about letting it go? By contrast, investment bankers take a strategic, objective approach. Our lack of emotional ties to the business allows for better negotiations and stronger advocacy.

In conclusion, the twenty-four percent higher valuation that investment bankers can achieve isn't magic, hype, or a marketing ploy. It's the result of experience, process, and skilled execution.

When you're selling your life's work, doesn't it make sense to have a professional in your corner, fighting to get you every dollar your company is worth? Remember, it's not just about making the sale—it's about making it at the highest valuation and on the best possible terms.

That's the difference a great investment banker makes. But handling complex deals requires more than just expertise—it requires mastery of the art of deal-making itself.

Let's explore the art of the deal more fully in the next chapter.

CHAPTER 9

LANDING THE TRIPLE LINDY

HOW INVESTMENT BANKERS MASTER COMPLEXITY

To illustrate the art of the investment banking deal, let me walk you through the most complex deal I've ever done. It involved five parties, with five legal teams, and we had only six months to complete the entire process.

My client named the project the "Triple Lindy." It's from Rodney Dangerfield's movie *Back To School*. In it, he creates a dive so complex that no student believes he can do it! And yet, he sticks the landing, and everyone goes crazy. In this chapter, we'll talk about how our firm manages complexity. If we stuck the landing on the "Triple Lindy" I'll describe, we can surely handle the complications your transaction presents!

Mastering complexity comes down to three things: prioritization, "On-The-Spot Execution" (OTSE), and a focus on "What Is Required to Close" (WIRTC).

Let's dive deeply into each of these crucial elements.

THE ART OF FOCUSING ON WHAT MATTERS

Prioritization is about having a filter to help you determine what you should focus on first. I often find that sellers struggle to solve complex issues. They don't understand a buyer's needs and goals. They can be focused on issues that are important to them emotionally, but not significant to accomplishing a transaction.

This is normal behavior that we all engage in—myself included! I frequently ask as a transaction moves forward, "What am I not prioritizing properly?" It's vital to step back and assess what matters most in moving the deal forward.

In our "Triple Lindy" deal, we had to prioritize which of the five parties' concerns to address first. We created a matrix of issues, ranking them by their impact on the overall deal and the urgency of resolution. This allowed us to tackle the most critical issues first, ensuring the deal stayed on track despite its complexity.

THE POWER OF IMMEDIATE ACTION

Issues often arise that have a role to play in a transaction. A typical reaction is, "Oh, we should schedule a call" or "We should meet to figure out what to do." I've learned that, often, the best thing to do is stop, assess the facts and the situation, and execute your next step. We call this "On-The-Spot Execution" (OTSE).

Now you might say, "Aren't you moving too quickly or making a decision rashly?" And the answer is no. If you try OTSE and can't decide, it shows you need more information. But many times, you'll find the resistance was a temptation to push the matter aside for later when really, upon examination, you know what the next step is. Sometimes, that next step might just be uncomfortable, or something you don't enjoy doing as much as other things.

This habit is powerful. It lets us decide and act. Or we can pause to see if there's a more significant issue that needs further examination before deciding. Clients have often praised our firm's speed. I believe it reflects our culture and our commitment to executing important tasks immediately.

In the "Triple Lindy" deal, we had a moment where two of the five parties were at an impasse over a key term. So, we skipped making a series of calls. Instead, we held a joint session, hashed out the issues, and found a creative solution that satisfied both parties. This OTSE approach saved us weeks of back-and-forth and kept the deal on its tight timeline.

KEEPING THE CLOSE IN SIGHT

The other principle that helps clarify prioritization is what we call "What Is Required To Close" (WIRTC).

In a complex deal—be it a full or partial sale, or a merger—issues can arise after the deal closes. As a result, buyers and sellers can become fixated on those issues to address after closing instead of staying focused on getting the deal done in the first place.

Of course, I'm not suggesting that you ignore what will happen after the close. However, you must prioritize those things *after* fixing the issues necessary to close the transaction. This may seem obvious and many ideas in this book may seem equally obvious. Yet over and over I have seen firsthand how a cloud of emotion can affect people's ability to prioritize. You must ask yourself what must be done so that a closing can occur. If an issue or decision clearly must be handled after the close, then put it in that category. Don't spend an inappropriate amount of time or energy on that issue right now. That issue will never be relevant unless the transaction closes first.

In our "Triple Lindy" deal, we constantly reminded all parties of the WIRTC principle. This helped us avoid many post-closing issues that could derail us. By focusing on what was needed to close, we navigated the complexity. We brought the deal to a successful conclusion within the six-month deadline.

OUTCOME BEATS PROCESS EVERY TIME

In his classic business novel *The Goal*, Eliyahu Goldratt stresses the need for great processes. The process must support the outcomes you seek. He tells of a company that struggled due to its factory's limitations. He shows how management overcame those constraints by becoming willing to adapt and change their process.

It turned out that some things that had made their process successful in the past were now impediments in the new environment. Now, having a great process is essential, but what's even more important is getting a great outcome!

Yet following processes too closely can sometimes lead to lazy thinking. A strict adherence to a rigid process may limit creative options. Those options might lead to better outcomes.

I'm amazed by some firms' often mindless adherence to their processes. Such rigidity often harms their clients. As I said, success must be defined solely on outcome, not on how precisely you adhered to a process which may not be best for a given transaction. That's the company equivalent of participation trophies, in my opinion! Instead, know the outcome you desire, and as a result, the process of how you get there becomes far less important.

Let's look at some examples from the worlds of business and sports:

Ilan Goldfajn, the former president of Brazil's central bank, once said, "The important thing is not the process, but the result." In his role as Brazil's leading banker, he focused on achieving economic stability. He did so even if it meant turning away from traditional monetary policy processes.

The New England Patriots, under coach Bill Belichick, were known for their adaptability. They didn't stick to a single playbook or process but instead adjusted their strategy each game to achieve a winning outcome. We all know what the Patriots accomplished—nine Super Bowl appearances and six victories in twenty years. The "Patriot Way" therefore could be summed up in a single word: flexibility. (And having a quarterback like Tom Brady!)

Stephen Curry of the Golden State Warriors revolutionized basketball with his three-point shooting. He didn't follow the traditional process of how a point guard should play, which until then meant initiating the offense as the "floor general." Instead, his focus on the outcome—scoring points—changed the game.

In each of these cases, the focus was on the desired outcome. It was never about following an established process. Mastering complexity in deal-making is about balancing prioritization, on-the-spot execution, and focusing on what's required to close. It's about keeping your eye on the desired outcome and being flexible enough in your approach to achieve it.

Whether you're facing a "Triple Lindy" level of complexity or a more straightforward transaction, these principles will help you navigate the challenges and stick to the landing.

To continue with our sports metaphors, when Bill

Belichick was coaching the Patriots, he didn't show all his surprise plays on the first drive. You thought you knew everything he had up his sleeve, until he unleashed a surprise play late in the game with the outcome on the line.

In negotiations, businesspeople sometimes make the mistake of putting all their demands up front. That approach doesn't work in the NFL, and it seldom works at the negotiating table.

In the next chapter, I'll show you why.

CHAPTER 10
THE MISTAKE OF UPFRONT DEMANDS
UNDERSTANDING THE TABLE STAKES FALLACY

In any negotiation, the "Table Stakes Fallacy" is the mistaken belief that you need to lay out all your demands in the first conversation. This approach can often backfire, leading to unnecessary tension and potentially derailing promising deals.

"I just want to be upfront with people and not waste their time," clients will tell me. It sounds reasonable and even honorable, but it can be extremely detrimental to getting the best outcome or even getting any deal at all. Let me explain why.

In the investment banking world, when it comes to raising issues and requests, timing is everything. So much of getting a deal done is about raising issues at the right moment and making sure everyone has the right context for the conversation. Sometimes a company owner will say, "If the potential buyer can't guarantee me these four outcomes upfront, I don't want to do the deal." Trust me—there's a time and a place for raising every issue you want to raise. You can always say no down the road.

The timing and context for any important issue is critical. In this chapter, we'll discuss the "Table Stakes Fallacy"—the idea that you must have certain things promised by buyers at the outset, instead of letting those issues arise at the right moment.

Before we dive more deeply into this concept, let's explore three crucial points that underpin successful negotiations in company transactions:

1. BUYERS NEED TIME TO UNDERSTAND WHY YOUR BUSINESS IS APPEALING

When you're selling a company, you'll naturally want to showcase all its strengths and potential in the first conversation, however buyers need time. They need to consider why you would be valuable to them. It's not a car race. You can gradually reveal your strengths and opportunities over time. Think of it as learning about a character in a great movie as the story progresses, or a conversation on a great first date. You don't want to give up (or learn) all the details right away! You want to preserve a little mystery, right? A discovery process can lead to a stronger emotional investment from the buyer, which can result in a better deal for you.

2. BUYERS ARE MORE FLEXIBLE AS YOU MOVE TOWARD CLOSING A DEAL

As negotiations progress and a deal seems more likely, buyers often become more willing to make concessions or accept terms they might have balked at earlier in the process. That's because they've already invested a lot of time and resources into this deal. They know the real value of the deal to them, so they'll be willing to give more ground to get it done. If you just hold back a few requests until later in the negotiation process, you may find buyers more receptive to giving you what you want.

3. SELLERS ARE MORE FLEXIBLE AFTER INFORMATION ARRIVES

Some things you may consider crucial on day one of a negotiation may not matter all that much in the context of the overall deal you are pursuing. At the outset of a sale process, sellers often have a list of "must-haves." These are conditions they believe are non-negotiable. But as the process unfolds and offers are on the table, sellers often reassess the importance of each condition. I recently had a seller laugh as he abandoned his prior "sacred cow" demand. He told me, "For this much money, I couldn't care less about that!"

This illustrates how perspectives can shift as the deal progresses.

THE POWER OF GENEROSITY IN CREATING ENTERPRISE VALUE

Generosity is a key part of creating enterprise value. As the ancient wisdom in Proverbs states, "The hand of the generous will prosper" (Proverbs 11:25), This principle applies not just to personal conduct, but to company strategy as well.

Companies succeed by wanting to deliver more to their customers. They aim to offer more value, better quality, and superior service. This same generous mindset can apply to deals. By understanding and taking to heart what the buyer needs, you can often achieve what *you* need.

There's an emotional currency in these deals. If you keep demanding small issues that matter to the buyer, you may not get what you want, like a higher price or better terms! A successful deal isn't about "My way or the highway." It's about "give-and-take."

That's why I invite my clients to understand the other party's view. Be flexible on less critical issues and create that wonderful win-win everybody wants.

A CASE STUDY IN PATIENCE AND FLEXIBILITY

Let me share a story that illustrates this principle. I once had a client with the longest list of upfront demands I'd encountered in my career.

One of his key requests was to keep his company's

website unchanged for five years after joining a larger group post-transaction. His firm had invested much time and effort in the website, and they felt it was crucial for gaining new clients.

The acquirer, however, was adamant. In their fifty-plus past deals, every acquired firm had quickly aligned its website and branding with the larger firm. On the issue of keeping the website unchanged for five years, the acquirer gave the seller a hard no.

I worried that this promising opportunity might be torpedoed by this single issue. I warned my client that he was asking the buyer to commit too early. It would require time, understanding, and patience to resolve the issue. I knew the acquirer and how they operated. I felt our best course of action was to be patient and focus on other issues. We needed to give the acquirer time to digest the website question.

When the time came, I recommended that we should ask the acquirer to explain its client acquisition strategy and how they would change the seller's website to fit their pattern. The acquiring organization was sophisticated. I felt certain that after they sought to craft a marketing strategy for the company they were buying, they would conclude that our approach was better than the one they came up with. And that's exactly how things unfolded. The seller was happy, and the buyer didn't feel as though he was making a concession to leave the website unchanged. He saw the value in what the seller was proposing.

The large, sophisticated acquirer began to work on a strategy to combine their website with my client's website. It soon became clear that making changes right away was a poor idea. They readily agreed to a significant period to bring the websites together gradually. Meanwhile, my client had gained a better understanding of the acquirer and became much more flexible in his approach to the transaction. He became excited about the future of the merged companies' marketing and website strategy.

I understand that it can be very uncomfortable to hold back demanding something you care about. You must have the patience for the other party to understand the issue. Call it strategic patience and it is a vital aspect of getting a deal done.

I often use a new romantic relationship as an analogy. If you ask for a marriage-level commitment just days after meeting someone, you may get a response like, "You seem like a good guy (or gal) but I just met you! What's the rush?" Wouldn't that turn you off if someone came on too strong, too quickly?

It's the same with selling a business. To get the other party to commit, you must give them time. They need to learn about your company and get to know you. Ideally, they should fall in love with your company and, if you plan to stay on, with you!

THE DELICATE BALANCE OF NEGOTIATION

To summarize, it's smart to have a list of things you want to accomplish. It's important to have clarity around the issues that are meaningful to you. But it's a mistake to push those demands too quickly into the negotiation. It's just a bad idea to start off by saying, "If you don't agree to these as table stakes, I don't want to engage." Nobody likes dealing with people who come across as inflexible! Where's the line between a deal-breaker and something that's just hugely important? Your banker, if skilled and experienced, can help you find that fine line. Your banker should also communicate with the marketplace about some of your goals. But your banker must not put parties on the defensive or make them say, "I don't know if we can agree to all of that. Let's just move on to a different and more flexible opportunity."

It's a delicate balance, but it's one that as a banker, I address all the time. We've found that, as we build the conversation and develop the relationship over time, we can engage on critical issues. We prioritize the timing of what matters most and gauge the other party's comfort with the company and its people. As a result, the buyer develops a sense of excitement about acquiring or partnering with the company.

In conclusion, remember that patience and flexibility can often lead to better outcomes in business transactions and don't fall into the trap of the "Table

Stakes Fallacy." Instead, build relationships, understand the other party's perspective, and let critical issues arise at the right moment.

As important as investment bankers are—and I think we're pretty darned important—we aren't the only member of your team as you explore a sale. So, let's explore how your current financial advisor can work hand-in-hand with your investment banker to maximize your success.

CHAPTER 11

HOW THE RIGHT ATTORNEY MAKES THE DEAL SUCCEED

After selecting a sound investment banker, choosing an attorney experienced in the sales of companies is crucial. I don't recommend using a corporate attorney with a general practice. You need an attorney who knows all about the art of the deal. I highly recommend coordinating this choice with your banker. An accomplished investment banker should be able to point you to counsel who can represent you effectively in a company sale.

CHOOSING THE RIGHT ATTORNEY

When selecting an attorney for your company sale, consider the following:

1. Experience in company sales transactions
2. Reputation in the industry
3. Understanding of your specific company sector

4. Ability to work collaboratively with your investment banker

The only person who will still be paid if the deal fails is the attorney. (Nice to be an attorney, right?) An attorney's view of things may sometimes not align with yours. An attorney once told me that the perfect legal risk outcome for him was a long negotiation that generated many billable hours but did not close. Why, you ask? If the deal does not close, all the legal work and documents created will never be challenged later, as nothing was signed and sealed. I found this thinking troubling to say the least, and of course I couldn't recommend that attorney, or his firm.

Choose someone who is experienced in transactions, has a reputation to uphold, and is actually happy when deals come to fruition. Paying your current business lawyer to learn during the process is very expensive and time-consuming. They shouldn't be learning how to do deals on your dime. You also want someone who knows how to manage the nuances and challenges that can arise at closing. An experienced attorney has seen these issues before and knows what to do to get a deal back on track.

COPING WITH THE "OH NO! MOMENT"

At the beginning of every legal process with the lawyers and accountants, I tell all my clients to expect the "Oh no! moment." This is when one of the lawyers or accountants comes up with a big problem that is usually brought up on a conference call rather than in an email. We solve these "Oh no!" problems all the time, and it's the job of those other advisors to raise important but often low-probability risks. Let me share an illustrative anecdote:

We were on a call once with our client and his lawyer, who had thirty-five years of experience and had been involved in hundreds of deals. He raised a serious-sounding risk and had no solutions to offer. My "Oh no!" radar was pinging. After troubling responses and questions from my client, I said, "Joe, you have so much experience in deals. In your over thirty-five years, how many times have you seen this happen?"

There was a long pause, and then he said, "Well, never, but it could happen."

My client immediately said, "This matter is closed, let's move on to the next issue."

MANAGING RISK AND EMOTION

Life entails risk. We all know that. However, when creating a transaction for the sale of all or part of a company, risk arises for both buyer and seller. So much of how we manage risk is related to emotion, and it's important to separate your feelings from actual risks. This comes through good legal counsel alongside counsel from your investment banker. Since they are the advisor and not the seller, it's easier for them to be objective about your deal.

I once had a case in which a legal point was debated back and forth for a couple of weeks between the parties. The issue was complicated, and both sides had some merit to their arguments. These cases are the most difficult because each party feels justified in their position and doesn't feel the need to back down.

I sat down with my client and went over the math behind the debate. It turned out that the dollars at risk were less than two percent of the proceeds he would receive. He and I agreed that the lawyers were going to struggle to find a solution, and the entire deal was being held up. He decided to accept the risk of losing two percent in exchange for achieving ninety-eight percent immediately.

TYPICAL DEAL STRUCTURES

As I've said, negotiation is a "give and take," not a "winner takes all" proposition.

So you and your team need to know what you can give up and what to insist on, to maximize the outcome and minimize risk. Let me explain how deals typically get structured in M&A. There are three main ways we typically see deals structured:

The first and simplest is **all cash at closing**. You get your full payment right away, clean, and straightforward. But here's what I've learned after decades of doing deals: buyers often offer less in all-cash deals, because they're taking on all the risk upfront.

Second are what we call **deferred payment deals**. Here, the buyer puts most of the money down at closing and then pays the rest over the next year or two, assuming your company maintains its performance. This gives both sides some protection.

Finally, the third option is **an earnout structure**. This structure is often misunderstood and avoided, but it can work well when done right. The seller gets a substantial payment upfront, plus the opportunity to earn even more by growing the company. Buyers like this approach because they're only paying more if the company performs.

I often hear criticism of this third approach. People say, "Well, no one ever gets their earnout." That isn't true. I have had many clients get their earnouts. The key to deal structuring is not to succumb to dubious rules of thumb like "Don't consider an earnout; no one ever gets them."

An attorney once gave my client this inaccurate advice, which caused him to resist the deal. It took a while, but I finally got them both on the phone. I explained that the earnout offer also offered the highest amount of cash at the closing of any offer, so any income received through an earnout would be a bonus. Of course, the attorney said, "Yeah, well that makes sense," but his knee-jerk rule of thumb—"Earnouts are bad"—clouded things unnecessarily for my client.

Beware of friends and advisors with arbitrary, unproven rules of thumb and their "stories." Look at the facts objectively with your investment banker and talk through scenarios. Make an informed decision based on the terms and conditions of your own transaction.

LEGAL RISKS OF DIFFERENT STRUCTURES

Your risk for future issues after a sale is strongly governed by how well you define what happened in the past and what assertions you make in the documents. This is one of the more crucial areas of your attorney's work. Most companies that are sold don't have past events that will bring the sale into question, but that can occasionally happen. For example, in an asset sale, the buyer purchases individual assets and liabilities rather than the entire company. This structure can benefit buyers as it allows them to choose which assets and liabilities they want to acquire, potentially leaving behind unwanted liabilities.

However, in an equity sale, a buyer purchases the entire company, including all assets (equity, land, etc.) and liabilities including debt. This is often simpler from a transaction perspective but may come with more risk for the buyer. When a deal like this transpires, the buyer typically assumes all existing contracts and licenses.

Selling a company isn't as simple as selling a house.

You can't use your brother-in-law's attorney to sell your company! As I've said, having the right attorney who understands company sales transactions is crucial. Remember to balance risk management and look at the entire picture when making decisions. You don't have to win on every issue to have a successful sale. In fact, if you try to win everything, you'll likely turn off the buyer and lose the opportunity to sell.

We've now talked about the roles of the financial advisor and the attorney in the sale of a company. Now, let me share the precise playbook we use to turn these complex pieces into successful deals in the next chapter.

CHAPTER 12
THE RCG PLAYBOOK
HOW SELLING PART OR ALL OF A COMPANY REALLY HAPPENS

As we have discussed, of the most critical aspects of a successful company transaction is having a structured, reliable process. This "playbook" allows a company owner to navigate complex financial decisions with confidence and clarity. At Republic Capital Group, we know a solid foundation is key for every engagement. Of course, customization adds real value.

THE BALANCE OF PROCESS AND CUSTOMIZATION

Many investment banks claim their processes make them unique. They highlight their discipline and consistency in handling transactions. Yet a defined process without flexibility will often fall short. As we've seen, rigidity doesn't guarantee value or meet individual needs. This is where customization is vital because it leads to better outcomes and service than a standard method.

An investment bank without a process should be a concern for a seller. Similarly, an investment bank that can't or won't adapt its process to meet your goals is undesirable. They're putting their convenience over getting you the best outcome. The ideal bank offers a clear plan but also understands each company is unique. I'd like to think that Republic Capital Group stands out by blending structure with flexibility.

Let me share with you our core fourteen-step process from initial meeting to closing. I hope that it provides you with the essential clarity we discussed at the beginning of this book and gets you excited about taking the journey toward selling all or part of your company.

STEP 1:
IN-PERSON MEETING

We always start with a face-to-face meeting. Video conferencing, Microsoft Teams, and Zoom are great tools, but they are also wholly insufficient to understand, appreciate and connect with someone we want to serve. Call us old school, but we want to invest the time and resources to come meet you in person. Selling your company is too important to leave to a talking head on a Zoom screen! From our perspective, your comfort outweighs our convenience.

STEP 2:
ENGAGEMENT LETTER

We initiate a project by signing an engagement letter with the client. This document outlines the project's plans and terms. It includes legal provisions for mutual protection and acknowledgments. This document should be thorough and well-defined, covering all the legal and financial terms of the engagement. The engagement letter may be longer and more complex than some prefer, but they're developed to address specific scenarios in the deal and needs of the client.

Beware of groups that offer a loose affiliation with minimal commitment. For example, if a firm suggests signing a one-page document that only outlines how they get paid, that's a sign that they may not have your best interests at heart. A typical engagement agreement should be twelve to fifteen pages long and should address every aspect of the relationship in detail.

For instance, our engagement letter includes provisions that protect us if you provide fraudulent information, or an issue arises during the transaction. These are low-probability events but must be addressed legally. Also, the agreement must state that the firm represents you and no one else. Unfortunately, I've seen situations where "consultants" advised both parties in a deal without knowing. That's a conflict of interest we would never tolerate.

Another typical clause is a provision that says if you terminate the engagement but still complete a transaction with a party we introduced within twelve to eighteen months, we are still entitled to compensation. This protects the bank from being cut out after doing the arduous work of finding and negotiating with a buyer. However, be wary of firms that try to extend this protection with any buyer for two years or more. This is excessive and not in your best interest.

STEP 3:
COLLECTING AND ORGANIZING INFORMATION: SETTING UP FOR SUCCESS

After the engagement letter is signed, the next step is collecting and organizing all relevant company information. This includes financial statements, operational details, and strategic plans. I'm a stickler for how this information is managed. At Republic Capital Group, we ensure that all sensitive data goes into a premier data room. Why? Because the security and organization of your data are critical.

Next, we provide the company with a list of all the financial information we need. At Republic Capital Group, we assist in organizing raw data for our clients. We also ensure that our security process protects confidential data from hackers or breaches. We don't use email communications when sharing sensitive documents. Instead, we use a data room or a central hub for all documents. We can track and control access when potential investors or buyers show interest. This includes watermarking any downloaded documents.

Here's an example: an investment banker from another firm once bragged to me that he only paid twenty-five dollars monthly for his data room. Our firm, on the other hand, pays thousands annually for ours. The difference is in the level of security and the protection of our client's confidential information. Which one do you think provides more peace of mind?

STEP 4:
PREPARATION OF MARKETING MATERIALS

We then dig into the client's company. We build financial models that tell the company's financial story. We prepare a Confidential Information Memorandum (CIM). This detailed document includes an overview of the company, its leaders, and its finances. This "book" is for pre-qualified investors or buyers who will eventually sign a Non-Disclosure Agreement (NDA) and are suitable for engagement.

STEP 5:
BUYER IDENTIFICATION, MARKET OUTREACH, AND INITIAL TALKS

Identifying the right buyers is one of the most critical steps in the process. This is where our extensive network and market knowledge will come into play. We create a strategic list of potential buyers and investors, then develop a tailored outreach strategy. Maintaining confidentiality is paramount during this stage. We control the flow of information to ensure that only serious buyers gain access to sensitive data. This helps separate tire kickers from those who are genuinely interested.

STEP 6:
THE TEASER AND CONFIDENTIAL INVESTMENT MEMORANDUM (CIM)

The next step is creating a teaser—a high-level document highlighting the opportunity without revealing identifying information about your company. The teaser should be vague enough to maintain confidentiality but intriguing enough to generate interest.

Once we identify serious buyers, we create a Confidential Information Memorandum (CIM), a detailed twenty-five to forty-page document with comprehensive information about your company. No one sees this document until they have been approved and have signed a Non-Disclosure Agreement (NDA). Once they've signed the NDA, they will also be given access to our data room.

STEP 7:
LAUNCHING THE SIXTY-DAY-OR-LESS CONFIDENTIAL AUCTION PROCESS

A crucial part of creating value is having a confidential and competitive auction process. This means we will engage the market and give them a deadline by which to submit a written Letter of Intent (LOI). This is important because it brings structure and control to the process. We customize the timeline of the process to sixty days or less about ninety percent of the time. It would be tempting to make it a cookie cutter process to some firms but not Republic. Sometimes sixty days can be too long for certain companies and situations and occasionally it makes sense to have a longer process.

EARLY TALKS AND PRE-SCREENING

After getting initial information, Republic will have a to call with potential buyers or investors. We ask questions and set expectations to pre-screen the field. This ensures everyone is on the same page about the deal. We know how to ask questions to understand their focus and save our clients' time. We also ensure they understand our client's business fully, so their valuable time isn't wasted educating them if they progress in the process. The key aspect of this is that we are using our skill and experience to begin to direct these prospective firm to the type of outcome you and we have agreed upon. Anyone who doesn't express openness to these goals doesn't progress in the process. For example, this prevents spending two months engaging with someone only to learn they want to buy your entire company while you only want to sell a minority position.

STEP 8:
INTRODUCING THE CLIENT

After a few conversations, if we see meaningful interest and a strong alignment of goals, we set up a call with our client. We advise our clients to let the potential buyer or investor explain their fit, rather than pitching themselves or their company. This approach encourages a natural discussion about strategies and alignment and most importantly, keeps our client from being in the position of chasing or trying to sell someone. There will be a time to pursue or close an interested party but this is not it.

STEP 9:
SIGNS OF INTEREST

After these talks, we ask for a non-binding Indication of Interest (IOI). This document includes the buyer's valuation of the seller's company and deal terms. It covers key financial aspects but not all details. This step is vital to see if their valuation matches our client's expectations.

STEP 10:
MANAGING THE DUE DILIGENCE PROCESS

Once a buyer expresses serious interest, the due diligence phase begins. This is where they closely examine every aspect of your company—operations, financials, legal standings, and more. Due diligence can be a taxing process, requiring considerable time and resources. Our role is to manage this phase efficiently, organize the data room, and act as an intermediary to handle buyer inquiries so you can continue running your company without disruption.

STEP 11:
HANDLING MULTIPLE OFFERS

In the event of multiple compelling offers, we can repeat this process with some of the parties. Our client then compares different IOIs or LOIs. LOIs are usually more detailed than IOIs. With multiple offers, our client can decide which offer to choose.

STEP 12:
EXCLUSIVE TALKS

Once a preferred party is chosen and an LOI is signed, we move into exclusive talks. Here, our client only works with that party. We guide everything, including talks with lawyers and ensuring smooth progress.

STEP 13:
NEGOTIATING TERMS AND DEAL STRUCTURE

This is where the deal comes together—or falls apart. Effective negotiation requires flexibility, creativity, and a deep understanding of what's truly important to both parties.

We work closely with our clients to define their non-negotiable terms, explore various deal structures, and find a path to achieving their financial and personal goals. Whether structuring earnouts, setting contingencies, or mitigating tax implications, we ensure that every aspect of the deal is addressed with precision and clarity.

STEP 14:
FINALIZING AND CLOSING THE DEAL

The last step is to negotiate and finalize the Purchase Agreement, which is the last part of closing the deal. The hard work we've all done culminates in this final phase. As I've said, we coordinate with legal and financial advisors to finalize the terms, navigate any last-minute challenges, and ensure that all conditions are met for a smooth closing. At this stage, confidence and clarity are essential.

We're there every step, guiding our client for the best result. Our goal is to keep you informed and engaged, managing the details so that you can focus on the next chapter of your life. Once everything is agreed and signed, the deal closes.

PROCESS, CUSTOMIZATION, AND VALUE

This fourteen-point playbook I've shared for you provides a foundation—a starting point for every engagement. But what truly sets us apart is our ability to customize this process based on your needs and circumstances. All great coaches have playbooks. But it's their approach to coaching that sets apart the best of the best. Now that you know our fourteen-point process, I'll explain our approach to coaching our clients in the final chapter.

CHAPTER 13

ALL THE G.O.A.T.S HAVE COACHES: CAN WE BE YOURS?

Just as every championship team needs a great coach, you need a trusted advisor to guide you through your business's most significant moment. You and your company deserve nothing less. Success is rarely achieved in isolation. The best athletes—the Greatest Of All Time—those who reach the pinnacle of their careers—they all have one thing in common: they have great coaches. Whether in football, basketball, or any competitive field, having a coach is a hallmark of operating at the highest level and striving to win your "Super Bowl."

As a company owner considering selling your company or raising capital, you're at a critical juncture—perhaps the most significant moment of your professional life. It's your "Super Bowl" and like any championship game, you need a great coach to guide you through the challenges, keep you focused, and help you perform at your best when it matters most. That's where Republic Capital Group comes in.

Throughout this book, we've explored the complexities of selling a company, the importance of proper valuation, and the critical role of an investment banker in maximizing an outcome. We've shared success stories, cautionary tales, and strategies that can make or break a deal. Now, as we conclude, let's reflect on why partnering with us is crucial for your success.

THE URGENCY OF ACTION

The business world constantly changes; timing can make or break a deal. Consider the following: economic shifts can rapidly change company valuations. As we've discussed, the COVID-19 pandemic is a stark reminder of how quickly market conditions can change. In March 2020, thriving companies were suddenly struggling to survive. Conversely, some sectors experienced unprecedented growth. Your company value today may be different from six months from now. Meanwhile, technological advancements or new competitors can swiftly alter industry landscapes. We've already talked about the Blockbusters of the world—yesterday's category killers, today's roadkill. Most importantly, we know that life is unpredictable. Health issues, family needs, or other personal events can force rushed sales. By preparing now, you create options for yourself later.

THE COST OF DELAY

We had a client in the retail sector who decided to "wait one more year" before selling. During that year, e-commerce trends accelerated, and the company's valuation dropped by 30%. Don't let this happen to you.

Another factor to consider—running a company that you're no longer fully committed to is stressful. This lack of enthusiasm can impact performance, reducing your company's value. One of our clients described it as "dying a slow death." Don't put yourself (and the company you've spent decades building) through that unnecessary stress.

WHY REPUBLIC CAPITAL GROUP GETS BETTER RESULTS

Most investment banks will tell you they're different. Let me show you exactly how we operate at Republic Capital Group, based on our actual track record.

When we launched in 2015, we started with a clear focus on wealth management firms because we saw an unmet need. That focus paid off—by 2022 and 2023, we were advising on more wealth management assets than any other investment bank in our space, outside the Wall Street giants like Goldman Sachs and Bank of America.

Our approach was validated in 2019 when our Beverly Hills transaction won Financial Services M&A Transaction of the Year at the M&A Advisor Awards. Then, in 2022, we helped orchestrate the largest acquisition of a CPA firm in wealth management history.

The proof is in our track record. We've grown from our Houston roots to Rockefeller Plaza in New York because our results earned us a seat at the most prestigious table in finance. But we've focused on our "sweet spot"—privately held companies worth twenty-five million to $500 million.

CLIENT SUCCESS STORIES

Let me share some transactions that demonstrate what Republic Capital Group can do.

On the West Coast, we spent two years working with a firm to restructure their ownership, bringing key employees into the picture. The result? A seventy percent increase in value, twelve competing offers, and a final valuation topping $100 million—tripling their original value, all in six months.

Our Beverly Hills deal in 2019 put us on the national stage. It wasn't just another transaction—it won Financial Services M&A Deal of the Year at the

M&A Advisor Awards. Then came the deal I described earlier as the "Triple Lindy"—named after that impossible dive in the comedy film *Back to School*. Picture coordinating five different parties with five legal teams against a six-month deadline. We got it done.

In 2022, we topped even that. When a major firm wanted to expand its tax capabilities, we helped them acquire a CPA firm in what became the largest deal of its kind in the history of wealth management.

THE REPUBLIC CAPITAL GROUP PROCESS—A RECAP

At Republic Capital Group, there's no cookie-cutter approach—each deal receives its own strategy. The process starts with understanding your business—not just the numbers but what makes you special. Take that landmark CPA firm acquisition we closed in 2022. Sure, it became the largest deal of its kind, but getting there meant deeply understanding how tax services could transform the buyer's business model.

Before we approach buyers, we position your company for maximum value. That Beverly Hills deal didn't win awards by accident. We found ways to create value the marketplace was attracted to that others had not imagined. This creativity matters—having the ability to see beyond the present and what exists now versus what can be.

Then comes the complex work of negotiations.

With the "Triple Lindy" deal, we had five different parties with five separate legal teams, all working against a six-month deadline that couldn't move. Getting that deal done meant coordinating every detail, every signature, every agreement. It's the kind of complexity we handle regularly.

We stay with you through every step of closing. Whether it's meeting tight deadlines like we did on "Triple Lindy" or structuring groundbreaking transactions like Beverly Hills, we've proven we can navigate even the most challenging deals to successful conclusions.

Think about it this way: Every major deal we've closed started with someone sitting exactly where you are now, wondering if their exit could ever happen.

The Beverly Hills deal, the record-breaking CPA acquisition, the "Triple Lindy"—they all seemed daunting at the start. But having the right expertise at the table made them possible.

TACKLING THE EMOTIONAL JOURNEY

Remember there's something that doesn't show up in spreadsheets—that's the emotional weight of selling your company. Sure, the numbers are important. But do you know what keeps many owners up at night? They're wondering if they are making the right choice for themselves and their team.

As we've discussed, during every major transaction

we've handled, we've learned that the human element matters as much as the numbers. At Republic Capital Group, we've developed our approach by completing landmark deals in wealth management. The Beverly Hills transaction and record-breaking CPA acquisition taught us that success means looking beyond price and terms. It's about understanding what matters most to everyone involved.

YOUR NEXT STEPS

The best time to start planning your exit is now. You see, your exit will come at some point. Start now, even if you're not ready to sell immediately. Just knowing your options helps you sleep better at night. Working with an investment banker like Republic Capital Group gives you a significant edge. You'll gain valuable insights into your company's market position. This translates to millions of dollars down the road in most cases. Even if you're not ready to sell or find a capital partner, start preparing now. We can guide you in what buyers look for in today's market and the future.

Don't leave your company's legacy to chance. Just as every sports champion has a coach, you deserve expert guidance for your life's most important financial event. Republic Capital Group is ready to coach, strategize, and partner with you to achieve the best possible outcome for your company.

Are you ready to win your "Super Bowl"? Let's talk about how we can help you achieve greatness in your company transaction. The clock is ticking, and the best time to act is now. Reach out today, and let's start planning your victory.

FINAL THOUGHTS
CREATING WEALTH AND A NEW SENSE
OF PURPOSE IN YOUR LIFE

If you follow the suggestions I've made in this book and achieve that 24% *More* premium when you sell your company, your life will be very different! You will enjoy a new level of financial wealth, and the time to benefit from the financial success you've achieved. So, let's take a moment to discuss the deeper meaning of wealth.

A self-made billionaire I know once described wealth as "The ability to do anything I want, within reason." So, the question becomes, what do you want? Is it to buy armfuls of Rolexes, garages full of luxury cars, or memberships at the finest golf courses? There's nothing wrong with that, but the day you die, you'll be remembered most fondly by your Rolex and Ferrari dealers and the membership director at your club. Is that enough of a legacy?

I say it isn't.

The goal is to have not only financial wealth but the time and health to enjoy it. Beyond whatever we do for ourselves and our loved ones, there comes the question of purpose. Why are we here? It couldn't be just for our own gratification. As the expression goes, when we are all wrapped up in ourselves, we make a very small package!

Instead, with great wealth comes great responsibility. You now have the responsibility to further any purpose you have.

As we take leave of each other in this book, I'd like to challenge you to think about the way you will use your newfound wealth not just to enjoy yourself— although there is nothing wrong with that; but also, to serve and create great outcomes for others.

Have you considered how you will give back? You can donate large sums to the nonprofit of your choice. You can use the money to uplift your religious institution. You could start an orphanage in Ukraine or some other beleaguered location on our troubled globe. But the short of it is—you must do something!

Wealth without purpose is just a pile of green pieces of paper. It's only when we have a purpose that extends beyond ourselves that our lives truly take on meaning and significance.

It's said that money is like a magnifying glass on our character. If we are charitable when we have less, we will be able to give far more with the blessing of wealth that comes with the sale of a business. If we are stingy before the sale, we''ll be the same way afterward. We'll try to keep it all for ourselves. But as the expression goes, I've never seen a hearse pulling a U-Haul!

Naturally, I hope I have the privilege of meeting you and serving you on a transaction that will be life-changing for you and your loved ones. But let me ask you this: the lives of who else will change as a result of your newest level of success? Whom will you serve? What purpose will you live out?

There was a great golfer of the previous generation named Chi-Chi Rodriguez. He came from an impoverished background, made millions on the tour, and gave away a fortune. He loved to tell people, "What you take with you is what you leave behind."

So my last question for you is this: we know what's in it for you—now that you've reached this new level of success, what's in it for everyone else? What will you take with you, and what will you leave behind?

As I said in the beginning, 24% *More* isn't just about money, it's about maximizing your impact, influence, and purpose in this life. We would be honored to walk along side you on this journey.

I Look Forward to Hearing from You!

If you're interested in learning how Republic Capital Group
can help maximize the value of your company,
we'd love the opportunity to serve you!

www.ingramcontent.com/pod-product-compliance
Lightning Source LLC
Chambersburg PA
CBHW042120190326
41519CB00031B/7563